SUPER SUITE

N O T E :

This book is intended to be fun and informative. However, care should be exercised to ensure that the materials used are nontoxic, that proper ventilation is provided, and that caution is exercised in handling sharp tools or objects.

First published in the United States of America in 2002

by UNIVERSE PUBLISHING
A Division of Rizzoli International Publications, Inc. • 300 Park Avenue South • New York, NY 10010

2002 2003 2004 2005 2006 / 10 9 8 7 6 5 4 3 2 1

Printed in Hong Kong • Library of Congress Catalog Control Number: 2002107292

Designed by Paul Kepple and Timothy Crawford @ Headcase Design

Author Photo by Rudy Archuleta

SUPER SUITE

The Ultimate Bedroom Makeover Guide for Girls

✳ ✳ ✳ ✳ ✳ ✳

By Mark Montano

With Carly Sommerstein

Photographs by Matthew Rodgers

UNIVERSE

Contents

INTRODUCTION 08

BUYER'S GUIDE 128

Chapter One
Nora's Passage to India
10

Chapter Two
Sara's Stripe It Rich!
18

Chapter Three
Lauren's Desert Caravan
26

Chapter Four
Amanda's Black and White Modern
34

Chapter Five
Kristin's Victorian Suite
40

Chapter Six
Jennifer's Glamour Girl
48

Chapter Seven
Keisha's Southwest Roundup
56

Chapter Eight
Kaori's Flower Power
64

Chapter Nine
Morgan's Ultra Mod
72

Chapter Eleven
Jenny's Asian Medley
88

Heather and Crystal's At the Bazaar
80

Chapter Ten

Chapter Twelve
Talia's African Safari
96

Chapter Thirteen
Ria's Industrial Design
104

Chapter Fifteen
Alaia's Royal Treatment
120

Chapter Fourteen
Emily's French Flea Market
112

Acknowledgments

Dedicated to Dad and Mom

Who showed me how to paint, sew, and glue my world together.

Thanks to:

Tony&Tina Makeup ❀ Kathleen Jayes ❀ Arielle Eckstut ❀ Atoosa Rubenstein

Karen Ramsey ❀ Shawn Joswick ❀ Michael J. Paul ❀ Jamie Suh ❀ Scott Jaworski

All of the families who participated ❀ Lisa Labrado ❀ Shaye Strager

Introduction

"Rarely does a super teen occupy a super suite."

❋ ❋ ❋ ❋ ❋ ❋ ❋ ❋ ❋

I've been a designer for many years, having worked for a number of top designers before I opened my own boutique, where I make and sell clothes and accessories to everyone from hip downtown girls to rich uptown ladies. For my runway shows during Fashion Week, I've used every trick in the book to visually transform dozens of tall, skinny girls into ravishing goddesses of haute couture. Now I want to show you how to use the same simple tricks to turn your plain-Jane bedroom into your dream digs and the envy of all who enter your domain.

For this book I selected fifteen girls between the ages of twelve and eighteen. I talked to them about their hopes and dreams and together we remade their bedrooms into fabulous new spaces that reflect who they are as well as who they want to become. And you can do it, too. You don't need a ton of money—just a little know-how, a good eye, and, most importantly, trust in yourself. What looks right to you is what is right for your suite. Pick a color scheme you love and adapt it to any theme. Mix and match elements from different rooms and blend them together to create a whole new look—a mirror from one room, a table from another, and so on. And here's the best part: These rooms are so inexpensive and easy to complete that after a few months you can add to, subtract from, or completely change your room's look!

Getting Started

Before you start decorating your room, there are few things you should do:

❋ Tell your parents that it is a fact that when you create a great environment in your bedroom you will study more effectively, sleep more comfortably, and have a more positive outlook, allowing you to be more successful in life!!!!

❋ When they agree to let you redecorate, clean your room!!!!

❋ Throw away anything that you don't want anymore!

❋ Put all of your bric-a-brac in a box. When you are finished, put back only what works in your new room.

* Clean under your bed so you can move it easily if you need to.
* Remove any stickers on your mirrors, walls, and furniture.
* Clean out your drawers. Dressers are much easier to move when light!
* Have a sidewalk sale to get rid of your old stuff. Use the money to buy paint or pillows or a craft kit!
* Make a plan. Set yourself one task a day so you don't get overwhelmed by the process and give up before you get started!
* Pick light colors, rather than dark. They will make you feel happier!
* Pick colors that look good on you. For example, if you look great in light blue, you will look wonderful in a light blue room. If you look awful in green, you will feel awful in a green room!
* Gather all of the tools you think you might need to start creating your craft projects: glue, measuring tape, rubber stamps, color pencils, rhinestones, scissors, tape, glitter, tacks, nails, hammer, staple gun, buttons, ribbons, beads, straws, string, lace, needles, thread, paint, paint brushes, rubber bands, boxes, old picture frames, plastic flowers, sequins, glue gun, glue sticks, etc.

Remember if you have any questions about *Super Suite* or creating your room, go to markmontano.com and click on the "super suite" link. Keep an eye out for a "super suite starter kit" and remember, the dumbest question is the one that goes unasked. I'm here for you and happy to help.

Good luck!

Mark Montano

Chapter One

Nora's Passage to India

Hot Pink Armoire

Indian and Southeast Asian design has influenced Western culture for centuries, with good reason: it's feminine and glamorous, but still emphasizes the charm of handcrafting. Nora's room makes her feel like she is waking up in a palace every morning. "My friends are a little jealous! The pink fabric in the curtains diffuses the light and the whole room turns pink." After school, Nora enjoys hanging with her friends and listening to all kinds of music. Her best subject in school is English and she's a dedicated reader. She plans to study performing arts some day.

I'm Sari Canopy

Framed Hindu Deities

Lamp

Curtains

Throne

Framed Hindu Deities

This is the material list for one frame.

What You'll Need:

❋ **1 Indian picture (see RESOURCES for details)**

❋ **1 8" x 10" frame**

❋ **Plastic beads and jewels**

❋ **Spray paint (we used gold—see RESOURCES for details)**

❋ **Newspaper**

❋ **Glue gun**

❋ **Face mask**

1 Glue the plastic beads all around the frame.

2 Lay down your newspaper in a well-ventilated area, put on your face mask and spray paint the frame and beads gold. (Be sure to shake the can each time you spray and keep the can 8 inches from the surface you're spraying.)

3 When it has completely dried, glue on the jewels. (We found some great Indian illustrations in a book and color copied them for this frame. These look great when you place several in a row.)

Throne

What You'll Need:

* **1 old chair with detachable cushion seat (see NOTE below)**
* **1 Indian picture**
* **Plastic beads and jewels (we used yellow)**
* **Fabric (enough to cover seat)**
* **Sequins**
* **1 quart of high-gloss enamel (we used hot pink— see RESOURCES for details)**
* **Paintbrush**
* **Gloves**
* **Newspaper**
* **Clear-drying glue (like Elmer's)**
* **Glue gun**
* **Staple gun**
* **Screwdriver**
* **Needle and thread**
* **Scissors**

1 Unscrew and remove the seat from the chair. (If the cushion is attached to the stool with nails or tacks, save them so you can reattach the cushion later.) Lay out newspaper, put on your gloves, and paint the chair with the high-gloss enamel. NOTE: This paint is sticky and hard to get off, so use gloves! For cleanup, use mineral spirits on your brushes and nail-polish remover on your skin.

2 When the paint has thoroughly dried, attach the Indian image to the chair back with a thin layer of glue. Hot glue the beads around it to make a frame. We also used plastic jewels to make it sparkle.

3 Find a cool, crazy fabric that feels right to you and sew on a few sequins. Staple the fabric to the bottom of the seat and screw the seat back on to the chair. (If you're using a chair without a cushion, you can create a cushion using cotton batting; see the directions for the Tufted Headboard on page 44 for details.)

Your new throne is now ready for the most beautiful adornment of all—you!

Hot Pink Armoire

This takes time, but the results are gorgeous.
It's definitely worth it, and great for hiding clutter.

What You'll Need:

- ❋ **1 armoire**
- ❋ **4 Indian pictures (see RESOURCES for details)**
- ❋ **Plastic beads and jewels (we used gold)**
- ❋ **Oval-shaped plastic picture frames**
- ❋ **½ gallon of high-gloss enamel paint (we used hot pink—see RESOURCES for details)**
- ❋ **Spray paint (we used gold—see RESOURCES for details)**
- ❋ **Paintbrush and small paint roller**
- ❋ **Gloves**
- ❋ **Newspaper**
- ❋ **Clear-drying glue (like Elmer's)**
- ❋ **Glue gun**
- ❋ **Scissors**
- ❋ **Face mask**

1 Cover your work space with newspaper. Make sure your armoire is clean and dry, put on your gloves, and paint it with the high-gloss enamel. You may need two coats to cover the armoire thoroughly. Let the paint dry completely. NOTE: This stuff is sticky and hard to get off, so use gloves! For cleanup, use mineral spirits on your brushes and nail-polish remover on your skin.

2 If necessary, enlarge your Indian images on a color copier; make two 11" x 17" and the other two 8½" x 11". Cut them into oval shapes.

3 Once the paint on the armoire is thoroughly dry, attach the pictures to the doors with a thin layer of clear glue. Hot glue gold beads around their edges to create frames.

4 To create handles on the bottom of the armoire, glue beads onto the small oval frames. Open a window, put on your face mask, and spray paint them gold. (Be sure to shake the can well and hold it 8 inches from the surface you're spraying.) Hot glue the frames to the armoire.

5 Hot glue the plastic jewels between the ovals and to the center of the armoire. We also glued beads on top for additional sparkle.

Lamp

What You'll Need:

* 1 cool old lamp with shade
* 1 yard of fabric (we used blue)
* Ribbon (to determine how much you'll need, measure the base of your lampshade and add a few inches to give you enough to decorate the sides)
* Spray paint (we used gold—see RESOURCES for details)
* Plastic beads (we used gold)
* Newspaper
* Glue gun
* Pencil
* Scissors
* Face mask

1 Remove the lampshade.
Lay out your newspaper in a well-ventilated area, put on your face mask, and spray paint the base of the lamp. (Be sure to shake the can each time you spray and keep the can 8 inches from the surface you're spraying.)

2 Roll the fabric around the lampshade and trace the pattern. Cut out the pattern (leaving a little extra to tuck under and inside the shade), and hot glue the fabric onto the shade.

3 Cover any raw edges with ribbon, and don't be afraid to go a little crazy with the gold beads. In this case, more is definitely better!

Curtains

What You'll Need:

* 3 yards of taffeta (2 yards of one color, 1 yard of a different color; we used more pink than purple)
* Small sequin appliqués
* 2 yards of fringe (we used gold)
* Glue
* Hammer and nails
* Sewing machine or needle and thread

1 Measure your windows to determine how much fabric you'll need. This window treatment called for three panels that were 20 inches wide and 60 inches long. Two of the panels are hot pink and one is purple.

2 Finish the edges by folding over the raw edges of the fabric to create a ½-inch hem on the bottom and sides of the curtain. At the top, fold the fabric over 1½ inches to create a sleeve for your curtain rod. Straight stitch them using your sewing machine or hand sew them with ½-inch stitches. Sew the fringe on the top and bottom of the panels.

3 Glue the sequins to the panels.

4 Tack up the curtains with small nails (check with Mom or Dad first) or hang on a curtain rod.

I'm Sari Canopy

What You'll Need:

* ❋ 3 yards of light fabric (like chiffon) with an Indian flair
* ❋ Staple gun
* ❋ Ladder

1 Staple the fabric to the ceiling, letting it billow in between staples as pictured (check with Mom or Dad first). You'll need a friend to help with the positioning. And be careful up there on that ladder!

Resources for this Room

❋ ❋ ❋ ❋ ❋ ❋ ❋ ❋

PAINT: The room's walls were covered with Benjamin Moore Crocus Petal Purple 2071-40 in flat-finish latex. The throne and armoire were painted in Benjamin Moore Hot Lips 2077-30 high-gloss enamel. Krylon spray paint in gold, $3 per can.

BEDSPREAD: This was a real find: only $13 in a real five-and-dime store. Made of polyester satin, we liked its super bright pink hue. If you have a Chinatown near you, check out its home-furnishing stores.

LAMP: This was a great flea market find: only $5! Make sure any used lamp is in good working order before decorating and using it.

INDIAN PICTURES: Many communities have a "Little India" neighborhood or stores that carry Southeast Asian items where you can pick up beautiful and inexpensive images of Hindu deities or nature scenes. About $1 each.

RUGS: We found some great blue rugs to match the canopy. We used two in order to cover more floor. It's okay to use two small rugs instead of one big one, and it's often cheaper! You can always tape them together underneath.

ARMOIRE and CHAIR: We found the armoire at a Salvation Army store for $25; the chair was $10. Keep an eye open at flea markets, estate and yard sales, garage sales, thrift shops, etc. You'll find your pieces.

FABRIC: We used inexpensive polyester taffeta for the curtains, about $6 per yard. The chair fabric was also polyester taffeta with sequins.

MISCELLANEOUS: Sequin appliqués, gold plastic beads, plastic jewels, and plastic frames: 99-cent stores and craft stores sell these really cheap. Pick up a bunch and mix and match.

Chapter Two

Sara's Stripe it Rich

Padded Headboard

Bright colors make a room feel like it's jumping for joy. Lime-green, yellow, and light-blue paint, as well as some useful storage solutions, make this cozy setup vibrant and livable. Sara agrees: "The room seems so much bigger and more comfortable now. The storage boxes help a lot to keep my room clean." Sara's favorite parts of the room are the headboard and the pillows: "I wind up studying there with a portable laptop desk instead of sitting at my old brown desk." Sara's favorite things to do are hanging out, dancing, playing pool, going to the movies, and walking around the city with friends. She's on her way to college next fall, where she'll take classes in social work and education.

Wall Treatment

Light Fixture Cover

Bag and
Jewelry
Organizer

Ribbon Pillows

Rug

Wall Treatment

This is a great technique for a basement room or any room with low ceilings.

What You'll Need:

※ Flat-finish paint in two colors, one light, one dark (see RESOURCES for details)

※ Paint brushes or rollers

※ Gloves

※ Newspapers

※ Measuring tape

※ Pencil

※ Masking tape

1 Open up the windows to ensure good ventilation, lay down your newspapers, and find another place to sleep for the night!

2 Paint all of the walls with the lighter color of paint. Let it dry completely.

3 Using your measuring tape and a light pencil, mark off 22-inch-wide floor-to-ceiling stripes all the way around the room. Mark off the stripes with masking tape.

4 Paint every other stripe on the wall with the darker color. Let dry, and remove the tape.

Rug

What You'll Need:

※ 4' x 5' piece of upholstery fabric

※ 4' x 5' piece of canvas

※ Pins

※ Sewing machine

※ Double-stick tape

※ Scissors

1 Pin together the upholstery fabric and the canvas along their edges and across the center.

2 Sew with a sewing machine 3 inches in from where you've pinned. Remove the pins.

3 Make fringe around all four edges by cutting into the fabric about 2 inches every ½ inch or so.

4 Put double-stick tape on the bottom of the rug to keep it from slipping.

Light Fixture Cover

This is a cover for an existing wall sconce that needed a little updating.

What You'll Need:

❋ **About 25 inches of 1-inch-wide metal strapping**

❋ **1 yard of fabric**

❋ **2 wall screws**

❋ **Ribbon**

❋ **Screwdriver**

❋ **Needle and thread**

❋ **Scissors**

1 Bend the metal strapping into a semicircle.

2 Cut your fabric to fit the fixture (ours was 25 inches wide and about 20 inches long). Sew ribbon onto the 20-inch edges. Fold the fabric over 1½ inches to make a sleeve into which you'll slide the metal strapping.

3 Slide the metal strapping into the sleeve, re-forming the semicircular shape as you go.

4 Find the pre-punched hole in the metal strapping (under the fabric), place a screw inside it, and screw directly into the wall.

NOTE: If you remove the original fixture cover, remember to use nothing higher than a decorative 25-watt bulb; this fabric can be flammable.

Bag *and* Jewelry Organizer

What You'll Need:

- ❋ 3 coat-hanger bars (like you use in a closet)
- ❋ Spray paint (we used blue and white—see RESOURCES for details)
- ❋ Newspapers
- ❋ Screwdriver
- ❋ Screws
- ❋ Face mask

1 Lay down newspaper in a well-ventilated area. Put on your face mask, place the coat-hanger bars on the newspaper, and spray paint them. (Be sure to shake the can well each time you spray, and keep the can about 8 inches from the surface that you're spraying.)

2 After the paint is completely dry, attach the bars to the wall with the screws, and display your beautiful bags and jewelry with style. Seeing them will remind you to accessorize: the skill that separates humans from all other animals!

Padded Headboard

What You'll Need:

- ❋ 3 2' x 2' x 1/4" pieces of plywood
- ❋ 3 yards of fabric (we used a trio of 1 yard each of green, yellow, and blue)
- ❋ 3 yards of cotton batting
- ❋ Staple gun
- ❋ Scissors

1 Turn your bed lengthwise against the wall so that it's like a sofa.

2 Cover the front of all three pieces of plywood with cotton batting, stapling the edges to the back of the wood. Then cover the batting with the fabric.

3 Attach the plywood to the wall using a screw through the center of the wood. Make a tiny hole in the fabric where the screw will be placed. The weight of the bed will also help hold the headboard in place.

You can also add a horizontal wardrobe mirror above the headboard.

Ribbon Pillows

The following list tells you what you'll need to make one pillow. We made three in different colors. Be sure to multiply the amount of fabric, ribbon, and filling needed by the number of pillows you'd like to make.

What You'll Need:

✳ 2 yards of fabric per pillow

✳ 3 yards of ribbon per pillow

✳ 1 bag of pillow filling per pillow, or a cheap pillow from which you can remove the stuffing

✳ Needle and thread

✳ Scissors

1 For each pillow, cut 2 rectangular pieces from the fabric, about 30" x 20" each.

2 Stitch ribbons in stripes lengthwise across one piece of the fabric. You can crisscross the ribbons to create a plaid look.

3 Place the rectangles together inside out and sew them together, leaving a ½-inch of fabric on all the edges (this will give you a nice even seam all around) and a 5-inch hole.

4 Turn the fabric right-side out and stuff the pillow through the hole.

5 Carefully stitch the pillow closed.

Other Cool Stuff

Sara has a small stool that we spray painted to match her new décor. We also gave her cabinet a coat of glossy paint to update its look (see RESOURCES for details).

We made Sara's desk organizer out of multicolored collapsible boxes (see RESOURCES for details), and they went a long way toward organizing her work area. We were lucky to find these in just the right colors!

Resources for this Room

❋ ❋ ❋ ❋ ❋ ❋ ❋ ❋

PAINT: The room's walls were covered with Benjamin Moore Shimmering Lime 2030-50 flat-finish latex and Blue Bell 2064-60 flat-finish latex. For the cabinet: Benjamin Moore Clearest Ocean Blue 2064-40 high-gloss latex paint. Krylon spray paint in blue and white, $3 per can.

MIRRORS: To make your room seem bigger, use mirrors. We bought mirrors with different colored frames from Kmart; they were about $6 each. You can also paint them to match your color scheme. Place them across from windows and in the darker corners and watch your room grow!

COAT-HANGER BARS: We found these at a 99-cent store.

METAL STRAPPING: Available at any hardware store; the metal strapping costs about $1.50 a roll.

PLYWOOD: Available at any hardware store. Precut plywood costs about $5 per piece.

COLLAPSIBLE BOXES: We got these at The Container Store. They come in great colors and all different sizes.

FABRIC: We used inexpensive cotton fabric, about $3 a yard.

COTTON BATTING: The batting can be purchased at most sewing stores for about $3 a yard.

CLEANING TIP/HINTS: Spot clean the fabric headboard, light fixture cover, and pillows using Woolite diluted in water and a sponge.

Chapter Three

Lauren's Desert Caravan

Because Lauren is artistic, her mom let her write on her bedroom walls. It took a long time for us to cover all of the writing, but it was worth it. (By the way, if you have any pen marks on your walls, pick up a special paint called Stain Killer to cover them. If not, they'll keep bleeding through the new paint, no matter how many coats you apply.)

Lauren was delighted with the results: "It's like spending time in the desert. Everyone comes in and goes, 'Whoa!'" Lauren's favorite parts of the room are the bench—"I like to keep my stuffed animals inside"—and the lace curtains, which make pretty shadows when she uses the hanging candles. Lauren plays basketball and softball and loves listening to the radio. Her fave classes are social studies, geography, and English. She has also studied drawing and design.

Onion Dome Wardrobe Mirrors

Wall Treatment

Curtain / Window Treatment

Lamp

Hanging Screen Votive Holders

Dumpy Sofa Chic

Tassels (for pillows)

Magic Carpet

Onion Dome Wardrobe Mirrors

Have your mom or dad help you with the jigsaw, or try cutting the shapes out of cardboard instead of wood.

What You'll Need:

* 3 brown-framed wardrobe mirrors
* 3 pieces of plywood, 14" x 14" x ¼" thick (or to fit the width of your mirror)
* 1 quart each of light orange and terra-cotta high-gloss latex paint (see RESOURCES for details)
* Large sheet of paper (for tracing)
* Paintbrushes
* Gloves
* Newspaper
* Measuring tape
* Pencil
* Small jigsaw
* Hammer and nails
* Scissors

1 Create a stencil so all the domes will look alike: Fold a large piece of paper in half, and mark a point on the fold 12 inches from the bottom where the point of the dome will be. Then draw your dome and cut it out while the paper is still folded. When you open it up, you'll have two identical sides.

2 Using the pattern, trace the dome onto the pieces of plywood, and cut them out. If you don't have a saw, ask the folks at your local hardware store if they'll do it for you. (Take your wood home and trace it, then bring it back in to be cut.) Alternatively, you can use sturdy cardboard.

3 Lightly draw stripes on the domes as in the picture. Lay out your newspaper and paint the stripes with the orange and terra-cotta paint. (Note: We used a little bit of green at the top to make a cap and to pull in the color of the carpet.)

4 After we hung up the mirrors, we tacked up the onion domes on the top and the bottom using very small nails.

Tassels
(for pillows)

This is the material list for one tassel.

What You'll Need:
* 1 6" piece of cardboard
* 1 ball of yarn (your color choice)
* Scissors

1 Take the yarn and wrap it lengthwise around the piece of cardboard about 60 times. Slip a 6-inch piece of yarn through the top and tie tightly.

2 Cut the yarn apart at the bottom. Wrap a long piece of yarn around the top of the tassel, and tie in a knot. Hang or sew it to the corner of a pillow like we did.

Wall Treatment

What You'll Need:
* 1 gallon of sand-colored flat-finish latex paint
* 1 gallon of light orange flat-finish latex paint
* 1 gallon of deep orange flat-finish latex paint (see RESOURCES for details)
* Paintbrushes or rollers
* Gloves
* Newspaper
* Measuring tape
* Pencil
* Masking tape

1 Divide the room's walls in half horizontally using your measuring tape and pencil. Mark the dividing line with the masking tape.

2 Lay down your newspaper and open the windows to ensure good ventilation. Find somewhere else to sleep for the night!

3 Paint the upper half of the room in the sand color and the lower half with the deep orange.

4 When the paint is thoroughly dry, use a paintbrush to create the sandy hill scene by making a wavy line in varying thicknesses in the light orange color. Don't bother to trace this part. It looks hard but it's really easy.

We also painted part of the ceiling in the sand-colored paint to give Lauren something nice to look at when she was in bed. Who wants to look at a white ceiling when there's so much color everywhere else? It makes the room feel warmer.

Lamp

What You'll Need:

* 1 lamp with lampshade
* Spray paint (we used orange—see RESOURCES for details)
* Newspaper
* Face mask

1 Lay out your newspaper in a well-ventilated area, put on your face mask, and spray paint the base of the lamp. (Shake the can well each time you spray, keeping the can about 8 inches from the surface you're spraying.)

2 When it's thoroughly dry, add a lampshade that feels right for the room.

Dumpy Sofa Chic

This has got to be the easiest makeover ever for a sofa that has seen better days.

What You'll Need:

* 1 old small sofa
* 1 queen-size bedspread or throw
* Pillows
* Safety pins

1 Pick up an inexpensive queen-size bedspread or throw and toss it over the sofa, tucking it in around the arms.

2 Using safety pins, secure the bed throw to the back and sides of the sofa so it won't slip.

3 Add throw pillows for a whole new look!

Magic Carpet

What You'll Need:

❋ 1 piece of old carpet or carpet remnant (see RESOURCES for details)

❋ 4-inch-wide ribbon (measure the edges of your carpet to determine how much you'll need)

❋ Spray paint (we used silver—see RESOURCES for details)

❋ Newspapers

❋ Paper bag

❋ Pencil

❋ Glue gun

❋ Scissors

❋ Face mask

1 If you don't already have an area rug in your room that you'd like to rejuvenate, pick up a carpet remnant.

2 Next, make a stencil from a large paper bag. Cut the bag open to make it flat. Fold it in half twice, draw on the onion and bar shapes, and cut them out. You can use our design or any design that feels "desert-y" to you. (Consult an encyclopedia, design magazine, or website for ideas.)

3 Lay down your newspaper in a well-ventilated area, put on your face mask, place your stencil on the rug's surface, and spray paint it. (Shake the can well each time you spray, keeping the can about 8 inches from the surface you're spraying.)

4 Move the stencil and spray paint again. Continue to move the stencil and spray paint until you finish the rug, being careful not to smear the work you've just completed. To add color, you might want to paint the tips of the onions with a light blue paint, like we did.

5 Let the paint dry thoroughly (at least 1 hour), then hot glue some ribbon around the edges of the rug to finish it. Now you can fly away whenever you want!

Curtain/Window Treatment

Lauren has a loft bed that she wanted to be hidden and cozy. This works well for inexpensive bed frames that you don't mind marking with a staple gun.

What You'll Need:

* Polyester lace fabric (measure your bed frame to determine how much you'll need)
* Ladder
* Staple gun
* Scissors

1 Staple the fabric directly onto the frame of your bed (check with Mom or Dad first to make sure it's okay!).

2 Trim the fabric so it just covers the edge of your bed. If you follow the pattern of lace while you're cutting, you'll get a great, organic look that won't need sewing. You could do something similar to your windows. We also made two more Onion Domes on the wall next to the bed to create a little palace.

Hanging screen votive holders

The list contains the materials needed for one holder. Be sure to multiply the amount of screen and chain, as well as the number of candles and glasses, by the number of holders you'd like to make.

What You'll Need:

* 1 8" x 8" piece of window screen
* 4 8" pieces of small-link chain
* 1 20" piece of small-link chain
* 1 small drinking glass
* 1 votive candle (look for ones that say "non-drip" on the box)
* Pliers
* Hammer and nail

1 Use pliers to bend in the edges of your window screen a bit to avoid scratches.

2 Attach the 8-inch pieces of chain to the corners of the screen.

3 Attach the 20-inch piece of chain to the free ends of the 4 smaller pieces and cradle a small drinking glass with a votive candle in the center of the screen.

4 Hang it up wherever it looks great!

NOTE: Be careful where you burn candles. Make sure the area is clear of any flammable materials (like curtains) and always thoroughly extinguish a candle when you leave the room.

Other Cool Stuff

Lauren has her friends over a lot so she needed a place for them to sit while they hung out and painted each others' toenails. I put all of the things we didn't know what to do with in the trunk (page 29) and put a couple of pillows on top to make a comfortable seat. We also made curtains from golden yellow lace and made a bunch of extra pillows for Lauren's friends to hang out on.

Resources for this Room

✳ ✳ ✳ ✳ ✳ ✳ ✳ ✳

PAINT: We used Benjamin Moore Autumn Orange 2156-10 flat–finish latex for the bottom part of the wall, August Morning 2156-40 flat–finish latex for the hills, and Asbury Orange 2156-50 flat–finish latex for the walls and ceiling. We also used Benjamin Moore Calypso Orange 2015-30 high-gloss latex and Terra-cotta Tile 2090-30 high-gloss latex for the onion domes on the bed and around the mirrors. Krylon spray paint in orange and silver, $3 each.

WINDOW SCREEN: Available at any hardware store, about $1.50 per foot.

BED THROW: Ours came from Urban Outfitters, about $24.

PILLOWS: If you don't want to make your own, Ikea has some nice fabric-covered pillows that would look beautiful in this suite, about $15 each.

STORAGE TRUNK: The great-looking trunk came from Kmart, and it only cost about $20.

MIRRORS: These three wardrobe mirrors came from Kmart, about $7.99 each.

CARPET: The piece of industrial remnant carpet we used (try any carpet store) cost about $15.

LAMP: This one is from Urban Outfitters. It cost about $12.

SMALL-LINK CHAIN: We picked up the chain at the hardware store for 50 cents per foot. They'll cut it to the size you need.

Chapter Four

Amanda's Black and White Modern

Wall Treatment

Amanda enjoys spending time in her room now more than ever: "I never used to hang out in my room, but now I love it!" When asked if she ever tires of the black-and-white motif, Amanda shakes her head no: "When I add color to it, I just think of what will go nicely with black and white." Her new room has definitely inspired the more meticulous side of her personality: "I never like to have it messy, I always keep it clean and neat now." Amanda likes walking around with friends, as well as all kinds of music. Math and English are her best subjects. She wants to be an EMT some day.

Curtains

Amanda Pop
Art Poster

Lamp

Picture Frames

Amanda Pop Art Poster

What You'll Need:

❋ 1 or 2 of your favorite photos of yourself

❋ 1 black poster frame (size to be determined by your finished poster)

1 Take your photo(s) to any copy shop where you can gradually enlarge it to the size you want. Don't put the machine on the photo setting—just keep it at the regular setting. Enlarge the photocopies until they start to look very graphic.

2 Using many different-size copies, arrange the photos together in a collage and frame.

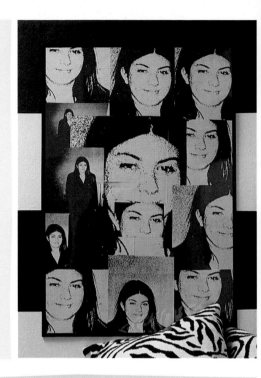

Curtains

What You'll Need:

❋ 2½ yards of cotton fabric, black-and-white striped, 30" wide (as used, right, for Lamp)

❋ Sewing machine or needle and thread

❋ Scissors

1 Turn the edges of the fabric under ¼" and stitch them with a sewing machine.

2 Have a friend help you staple up the material until you like the way it looks (check with your Mom or Dad first). Always start in the middle and staple outward toward the sides, leaving a drape.

Lamp

What You'll Need:

* 1 lamp with lampshade, white
* 1 yard of cotton fabric, black-and-white striped, at least 30 inches wide so you can use the same fabric for your curtains
* Black fringe (measure the bottom of your lampshade to determine how much you'll need)
* Glue gun
* Measuring tape
* Pencil
* Scissors

1 Remove the shade from the lamp. Roll the fabric around the lampshade, and trace the pattern. Cut out the pattern, leaving a little extra to tuck under and inside the lampshade.

2 Hot glue the fabric onto the lampshade.

3 Hot glue the fringe around the bottom of the lampshade.

Picture Frames

What You'll Need:

❋ 3 black picture frames

❋ Buttons, dominoes or any light, black-and-white objects you like

❋ Clear-drying glue (like Elmer's)

1 Arrange the dominoes or buttons into a pattern you like, and glue them onto the frames. Let dry.

2 Put your favorite photos in the frames.

Wall Treatment

What You'll Need:

❋ 1 gallon each of black and white flat-finish latex paint (see RESOURCES for details)

❋ Paint brushes or rollers

❋ Ladder

❋ Gloves

❋ Newspaper

❋ Measuring tape

❋ Pencil

❋ Masking tape

1 Lay out newspaper, open a window for ventilation, and find somewhere else to sleep for the night!

2 Paint the room white first. Let the paint dry, then measure out horizontal stripes with measuring tape. Draw lines and mark them with masking tape. Fill in every other stripe with black paint. (Trust us: It's much easier to paint black over white than white over black!)

HINT: Once your tape is on the wall and you're ready to do your stripes, go over the tape with white paint and a small roller. When that dries, paint black stripes. Your lines will be perfectly straight.

Other Cool Stuff

We replaced Amanda's rug with a simple white rug, 5' x 7'.

We sewed up some pillow covers in fluffy zebra fabric for the bed and found great zebra sheets to match.

We used two black, twin-size sheets sewn together to make a new duvet cover. You can use zebra or any black-and-white graphic, including polka dots, large stripes, or diamonds. It's much cheaper than getting a new duvet.

Finally, we placed three black-edged wardrobe mirrors next to each other on one wall to make the room look bigger.

We made an organizer out of kitchen baskets. They come in all different sizes, colors, and shapes, and they really help cut down on clutter while still allowing you to see what you are looking for. Just screw a hook into the ceiling and hang the baskets from the hook. (If it's not long enough, get some matching chain from the hardware store and make it longer.) Hang two or three for a really cool look.

Resources for this Room

❊ ❊ ❊ ❊ ❊ ❊ ❊ ❊

PAINT: Benjamin Moore Jet Black 2120-10 flat-finish latex and Benjamin Moore Cotton Balls 2145-70 flat-finish latex paint.

STRIPED FABRIC: Any fabric store will stock this fabric, about $4 a yard.

CHAIR: The Container Store supplied us with the ultra cool Umbra Oh Chair and bedside Luna Table. Go to www.thecontainerstore.com.

RUG: We bought the simple white rug at Kmart for $30.

WARDROBE MIRRORS: Target or Kmart sell these for about $10 each.

LAMP: We got this great lamp at Kmart for $9.99.

PICTURE FRAMES: The ones we decorated with buttons and dominoes came from Ikea, about $1 each. The poster-size frame came from Kmart, about $10. Try flea markets, thrift stores, or garage sales for slightly beat-up but usable frames.

CLEANING TIP/HINT: Use a Swiffer on the lampshade. It really works.

Chapter Five

Kristin's victorian Suite

Curtains

Picture Frame

The movie *Moulin Rouge* is one of Kristin's favorites, so the nineteenth-century feel of this room was a natural pick for her. This room may look complicated, but it really isn't. Just be sure to pick only a few colors and fabrics that go together, and stick with them. We chose blue tones with gold and fuchsia accents—tah-dah: instant glamour. Kristin couldn't have been happier with the results: "This room reflects who I am—kind of complicated and ornate." The canopy creates a private alcove within the room and Kristin reported that "the lamp casts a pink glow" throughout the room. Kristin keeps busy after school, volunteering at film festivals when she's not hanging out with friends in her swell new digs. A budding writer, Kristin plans to major in English one day, specializing in dramatic writing.

Hanging Lamp

Tufted Headboard

Table

Heart Pillow

Stool

Table

What You'll Need:

* 1 small table that you can use next to your bed
* Plastic beads (these could be "borrowed" from the family's Christmas ornament box, Mardi Gras leftovers, or any inexpensive beads that resemble strings of pearls)
* Spray paint (we used gold—see RESOURCES for details)
* Glue gun
* Newspaper
* Face mask

1 Place the table on your newspaper in a well-ventilated area, put on your face mask, and spray paint the table. (Shake the can each time you spray and keep the can about 8 inches from the surface you're spraying.)

2 Spray paint the beads, if desired. Once the table is dry, hot glue 3 different lengths of beads to the underside of the table so they hang in a graduated manner (see photo, left).

Heart Pillow

What You'll Need:

* 1 yard of taffeta (we used red)
* 1 yard of lace (we used gold)
* 1 bag of pillow filling (or a cheap pillow from which you can remove the stuffing)
* Paper
* Sewing machine or needle and thread
* Pencil
* Scissors

1 Create a pattern by cutting a heart shape out of paper.

2 Pin together 2 layers of taffeta and 1 layer of lace, and pin the pattern on top. Cut the heart shape out of the three layers. Sew the lace heart to one of the taffeta hearts.

3 Sew the two hearts together with the lace layer on the inside, leaving a ½-inch seam and a hole 4 inches wide. Turn the fabric right-side out and stuff with pillow filling. Stitch up the hole and *voilà*! You have a perfect heart pillow.

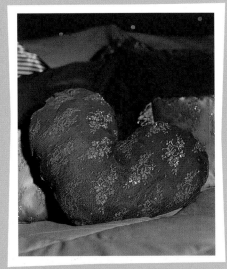

Hanging Lamp

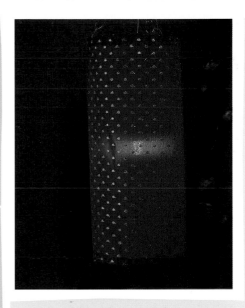

This one takes some time, but it's worth it! The metal strapping you use should have pre-punched holes, about one every inch or so.

What You'll Need:

* 62 inches of 1-inch-wide metal strapping
* 3 10-inch-long pieces of brass (or brass-look) chain
* 1 60-inch piece of brass (or brass-look) chain
* 1 yard of taffeta
* 1 yard of lace
* Light cord
* 25-watt bulb or lower
* Sewing machine or needle and thread
* String
* Glue gun
* Pliers
* Pencil
* Scissors

1 Cut 24" x 24" squares out of both the taffeta and lace. Lay one on top of the other and sew them together to make one piece of fabric; then sew the two long edges of that piece together to make a tube.

2 Create a circular base with the strapping by overlapping 2 pieces of 24-inch strapping, tying the two pieces together with string (utilizing the pre-punched holes). The circle should have a 23-inch circumference.

3 Place the metal strapping inside the fabric tube and fold the ends of the fabric over so they're tucked inside the circle. Hand stitch them on the top and bottom or use a glue gun to secure them to the inside.

4 Take the 3 pieces of 10-inch chain, and attach them to one another at one point—they should look like the legs of a spider—with the opposite end of each leg attached to the metal base. Look for the pre-punched holes, open up one of the chain's links, and secure it inside a hole with pliers. Attach the free ends of the 3 chains to the 60-inch piece of chain, from which the lamp will hang.

5 The last step is to attach your light cord (get this at the hardware store), string it down the chain, put in a 25-watt bulb and turn it on!

NOTE: Remember to use nothing higher than a decorative 25-watt bulb—the fabric can catch fire if it gets too hot.

Tufted Headboard

What You'll Need:

* 1 4' x 4' x ¼" piece of plywood
* 2 yards of 60-inch-wide taffeta
* 2 yards of cotton batting
* Measuring tape
* Staple gun
* Hammer
* Thumbtacks
* Straight pins

1 Wrap the cotton batting over the plywood, stapling it to the back side so the staples won't show.

2 Next, stretch the fabric over the batting, and again staple it to the back of the headboard so the staples are hidden.

3 Using the measuring tape and straight pins, mark the places where you'd like to create the headboard's tufts. Be sure to use the pins, not pencil, in case you change your mind mid-design. When you've decided, simply hammer in thumbtacks where you'd like indentations. We made a diamond, but you can make a heart or spell your name!

4 Attach the headboard using the directions on page 22.

Stool

What You'll Need:

* A foot stool or low table with detachable cushion seat
* 1 yard of taffeta
* 1 yard of lace
* Spray paint (we used gold— see RESOURCES for details)
* Newspaper
* Staple gun
* Screwdriver
* Face mask

1 Unscrew the cushion from the stool, and place it aside. (If the cushion is attached to the stool with nails or tacks, save them so you can reattach the cushion later.)

2 Put on your face mask, open a window, place the stool upside down on the newspaper, and spray paint it. (Be sure to shake the can well each time you spray, and keep the can about 8 inches from the surface you're spraying.)

3 While the spray paint is drying, place the lace over the taffeta. Using the staple gun, staple the lace and taffeta over the existing cushion. (If you're using a low table or a chair without a cushion, you can create a cushion using cotton batting; see the directions for the Tufted Headboard, left, for details.)

4 Reattach the cushion to the thoroughly dry base, using screws, or a staple gun or glue gun. You've got a whole new piece of furniture (and a great place to lay out tomorrow's school clothes)!

Picture Frame

This is a bit like the macaroni art you made in grade school, and it's just as fun.

What You'll Need:

* ❋ 2 pieces of cardboard (size determined by the size of your photo or piece of art)
* ❋ Pasta (we used elbow and penne—choose any shape you like)
* ❋ Spray paint (we used gold—see RESOURCES for details)
* ❋ Tape
* ❋ Newspaper
* ❋ Clear-drying glue (like Elmer's)
* ❋ Face mask
* ❋ Scissors

1 Take a piece of cardboard (we used one that measures 5" x 6") and cut a square from the middle that is a bit smaller than the photo you're framing.

2 Glue the pasta onto the frame with your clear-drying glue, arranging the pattern as in the photo here or in a design you prefer.

3 When the glue is dry, lay out your newspaper in a well-ventilated area, put on your face mask, and spray paint the frame. (Be sure to shake the can well each time you spray and keep the can about 8 inches from the surface you're spraying.)

4 Tape the photo to the back of the cardboard so it shows through the hole. Attach a piece of cardboard to the back to support and protect your art. Tack the frame to the wall wherever you choose.

Curtains

What You'll Need:

* ❋ 4 yards of fabric, striped
* ❋ 1 yard of lace
* ❋ 3 yards of fringed trim
* ❋ Staple gun

1 Staple the striped fabric around the window. Be creative!

2 Drape the lace over the striped fabric.

3 Using the staple gun, add fringed trim for flair.

Other Cool Stuff

We added a 5' x 6' pink rug to lighten the room.

We spiffed up a lot of the things Kristin already had, including spray painting her picture frames and mirrors to match the new décor. Kristin already had a canopy in her room. We covered it with five yards of gold fringed lace. We made long tubes of blue sparkly fabric to cover the frame and then made vines from fake flowers. We sprayed the vines gold and wrapped them around the poles. If you want to get this look but don't have a canopy, you can just hang vines from the ceiling down to the corners of your bed! It's easy and gives you the same feel.

We also organized Kristin's extra stuff on one shelf so the room looked neater. And of course, we added a lot of extra pillows. Nothing says "welcome to my suite" like pillows.

Resources for this Room

❋ ❋ ❋ ❋ ❋ ❋ ❋ ❋

PAINT: We used only one color in this room, Benjamin Moore Ultra Sky 2065-40 in flat-finish latex. Krylon spray paint in gold, $3.

PLYWOOD: Available at Home Depot, cut to your specifications, about $5 per piece.

TABLE and STOOL: Take a look in the attic for old furniture or keep an eye open at flea markets and thrift stores for slightly beat-up wood furniture that can be easily painted and re-covered.

METAL STRAPPING: This comes from the hardware store, about $1.50 a roll.

LIGHT CORD: Pick one up at Ikea or any hardware store for $6.

PLASTIC BEADS, FLOWERS and VINES: Available at most 99-cent stores.

FABRIC: The polyester taffeta we used is both inexpensive and durable, about $4 to $5 per yard. The lacey fabric used for the canopy was $10 per yard.

COTTON BATTING: Batting can be purchased at most sewing stores for about $3 per yard.

PASTA: Raid your kitchen cabinets or pick some up for a few bucks at any supermarket.

CLEANING TIP/HINT: If the plastic flowers and vines begin to get dusty, try cleaning them with a Swiffer, which pulls the dust away from the flowers without knocking them off.

Chapter Six

Black and White Poster Headboard

Jennifer's Glamour Girl

This bold room makes a big impact. Jennifer couldn't be happier with the results: "I really like things from the fifties. When friends come for a visit, this room makes that pretty clear. So having this décor explains who I am." She likes the new colors, and the way the stripes make the walls look taller. Jennifer's favorite things to do in her new super suite are reading and drawing. Her best subject is art, and she loves languages; she's currently studying Italian. Besides school, she's into hanging out with friends and going to the movies.

Powder Puff Jar

What You'll Need:

❋ **1 clean glass jar with lid (we used an olive jar)**

❋ **1 powder puff (to match jar size)**

❋ **Glue gun**

1 Make sure your jar is clean by soaking it in dishwashing detergent overnight or running it through the dishwasher.

2 Glue a powder puff to the lid.

3 Fill the jar with hairpins, barrettes, or anything else you can think of for instant dresser-top glamour!

Feather Mirror

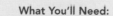

What You'll Need:

❋ **1 mirror tile**

❋ **Feather boa (measure the perimeter of your mirror to determine how much you'll need)**

❋ **1 piece of cardboard, 2 inches larger than your mirror tile all around**

❋ **Measuring tape**

❋ **Glue gun or clear-drying glue (like Elmer's)**

❋ **Hammer and small nails**

❋ **Scissors**

1 Measure the edges of your mirror to determine how much feather boa you'll need. Use sharp scissors to trim the boa and seal the cut with a bit of glue.

2 Glue your mirror tile to the cardboard; you should have two inches of cardboard showing around the entire mirror.

3 Glue the feather boa to the cardboard edges. Let dry.

4 Attach mirror to the wall by tacking through cardboard edges with small nails.

Curtains

What You'll Need:

* ❋ 2 pieces of satin in contrasting colors
* ❋ Measuring tape
* ❋ Sewing machine or needle and thread
* ❋ Scissors

1 To determine how much fabric you will need, measure the width and height of your windows (the windows shown here were 8 feet long).

2 Cut the fabric in 20-inch-wide strips and sew the strips together in alternating stripes. (We used three stripes of each color.)

3 Sew a sleeve along the top to fit the curtain rod and hang.

Fringed Rug

What You'll Need:

* ❋ 1 rug remnant (we used one about 30" x 60"; any color you like)
* ❋ Upholstery fringe (measure your remnant to determine how much you'll need; choose a color that complements your rug)
* ❋ Paper, Black marker, Pins
* ❋ Measuring tape
* ❋ Glue gun
* ❋ Heavy scissors

1 Create a pattern for your rug by tracing the size and shape onto paper. We took a pink carpet remnant from a carpet store that was about 6 feet long and 3 feet wide. We then rounded out the edges to make it look like an oval.

2 Secure the pattern to your rug with pins and cut it out with heavy scissors.

3 Hot glue the fringe around the edges.

Feather Lamp

What You'll Need:

* 1 small lamp, with lampshade
* 1 feather boa (we used pink)
* Glue gun
* Soft tape measure or long piece of string
* 25-watt bulb or lower
* Scissors

1 Run your tape measure or piece of string around the lampshade to determine how much of the feather boa you'll need. Use very sharp scissors to cut the boa; seal the cut with a bit of glue.

2 Carefully hot glue the feather boa around the shade.

NOTE: Use a 25-watt bulb or lower. Be sure no feathers are touching the bulb—they are flammable.

Fringed Sausage Pillow

What You'll Need:

❉ 1 24" x 46" piece of fabric (we used satin to match the comforter—see RESOURCES for details)

❉ ½ yard of coordinating ribbon

❉ 1 yard of coordinating fringe

❉ 1 bag of pillow filling (or a cheap pillow from which you can remove the stuffing)

❉ Sewing machine or needle and thread

1 Sew fringe along the two shorter (24-inch) sides of your piece of fabric.

2 Sew the 46–inch edges together to make a long tube.

3 Fill the tube with pillow stuffing, leaving about 6 inches empty at each end.

4 Tie the ends with ribbon about two inches from the fringe and you're done! (Hint: Make sure the knot is really tight or some of the stuffing may ease its way out over time.)

Wall Treatment

What You'll Need:

* 1 gallon each of white, gray, and pink paint (see RESOURCES for details)
* Paintbrushes or rollers
* Gloves
* Ladder
* Newspapers
* Measuring tape
* Pencil
* Masking tape

1 Lay down your newspaper and open the windows for ventilation. (You'll need to find somewhere else to sleep for the night.)

2 Measure a line around the room about 41 inches from the floor, and mark with masking tape.

3 Paint the wall white above the line.

4 After the paint dries, tape off vertical stripes above the line (each about 22 inches wide), and paint, alternating white and gray.

5 After your stripes are dry, mark a line on the wall 41 inches from the floor and paint the wall below it pink.

Resources for this Room

❋ ❋ ❋ ❋ ❋ ❋ ❋ ❋

PAINT: Benjamin Moore Light Chiffon Pink 2000-60 flat-finish latex, Benjamin Moore Spring Violet 2117-50 (gray) flat-finish latex, and Benjamin Moore Dreamy Cloud 217-70 (white) flat-finish latex.

CARPET REMNANT and FRINGE: We picked this one up at a carpet store for $10. The fringe cost $5.

MIRROR TILE: An 8" x 8" mirror tile costs about $3 at a hardware store.

LAMP: Ours came from Kmart and cost $9.99.

POSTER FRAME: From Kmart, about $9.99.

FEATHER BOA: Available at most fabric and trimmings stores, boas are roughly $10 to $14 for 72 inches, depending on the type of feathers you desire.

SATIN FABRIC: We used about 6 yards of inexpensive polyester satin for the curtains and 1 yard for the pillow; the total cost was about $40. You can find it for less.

CLEANING TIPS/HINTS: To clean dust from the mirror and other boa-bestowed items, shake—don't rub—the feathers. Hand wash the curtains and pillows; they'll last longer that way.

Chapter Seven

Keisha's Southwest Roundup

Twig Magazine Rack

Wall Treatment

CD Rack

After living with the changes to her room for many months, Keisha still loves it: "I really like the room this way. I especially like the 'Eye of God' hanging in the window. It's really pretty when the light hits it." She says her room was too crowded before, but now it has more balance—which is something that her mom appreciates, too. Keisha's favorite thing to do after school is hanging out with her friends. She's interested in studying fashion one day.

Rope Wall Detail

Eye of God

Bean Art

Rope Frame

Bean Box

Tin Table

Clay Pot Lamp

Tin Table

What You'll Need:

* 1 small unfinished wood table (or you can make your own with unfinished pine board like we did)
* 1 sheet of easy-to-cut (thin) sheet metal (measured to fit your tabletop)
* Shears or heavy scissors
* Canvas gloves
* Nails in various sizes or thumbtacks
* Hammer
* 1 cup of turquoise flat-finish latex paint, watered down (see RESOURCES for details)
* Sponge
* Newspaper
* Rag

1 Put on your canvas gloves so you don't cut yourself! Spread out your sheet metal and cut out a piece big enough to cover your tabletop.

2 Tap in tacks and small nails around the edges of the metal to keep it down.

3 Choose a motif for your table-top design. Using a variety of large and small nails and thumb-tacks, tap in the design. We hammered in tons of nails and tacks in cool patterns all over the table. You can do anything you want—write your name, make hearts and squares, create a floral or wildlife design, and so on.

4 Now lay down your newspaper, water down some turquoise wall paint (use two parts paint to one part water), and sponge it on the wood to give it a stained look. While the paint's still wet, wipe off any drops that may have hit the metal. Let dry thoroughly before placing items on the tabletop.

Rope Frame

What You'll Need:

- ❋ 1 wooden picture frame
- ❋ Rope (measure your frame to determine how much you'll need)
- ❋ Measuring tape and scissors
- ❋ Glue gun or small nails and hammer

1 Glue (or tack on with tiny nails) the rope to your picture frame.

Other Cool Stuff

We found a cool Southwestern-style rug and put some dried flowers in a clay vase. We made pillows out of fabric with a Southwestern flair and used mix-and-match sheets to pick up all the colors of the room.

To give Keisha's bed a more Southwestern feel, we used a mat of willow twigs and tacked it over her existing headboard. You can also use long twigs to hang simple curtains.

Resources for this Room

❋ ❋ ❋ ❋ ❋ ❋ ❋ ❋

PAINT: Benjamin Moore Coral Spice 2170-40 flat–finish latex and Benjamin Moore Turquoise Powder 2057-50 flat-finish latex.

ROPE: We got ours from the hardware store; $6.99 for about 20 feet.

DRIED PEAS and BEANS: Any supermarket has them, about $2 per bag.

CLAY POT: This simple pot came from the garden department of Kmart; about $3.

LIGHT CORD: Pick one up at Ikea or the hardware store for $6.

SHEET METAL: Find any hardware store, about $2.50 for 1 foot. An alternative to sheet metal is soda cans: carefully cut them open and flatten them (be sure to wear canvas gloves!); you'll need about 6.

TWINE: Available at any hardware store, about $2 per ball.

PINE BOARDS: Cut to measure at Home Depot. All the wood used in this room cost about $25.

CLEANING TIP/HINT: Use a Swiffer on the bean and twine items and clay pot lamp; it will pick up the dust without disturbing your decorations.

Chapter Eight

Kaori's Flower Power

Floral Headboard

Satin Pillows

If flowers are your thing, this room throws a flower-power knockout punch. Kaori worked for a florist one summer so she loved the idea of transforming her minimalist bedroom into a flower suite. "It's so much fun waking up in this pink and green garden! It makes me feel like every day is summer." Kaori's favorite things to do are water ski-ing, drawing, and shopping. Her favorite subject in school is art. She would like to be a clothing designer one day.

CD Rack

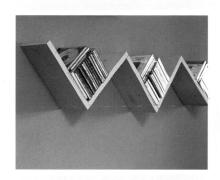

What You'll Need:

* ❋ 4 6" x 12" x 1" pine boards
* ❋ Wood glue
* ❋ 1 cup of coral flat-finish latex paint, watered down (see RESOURCES for details)
* ❋ Paintbrush
* ❋ Newspaper
* ❋ 3 mounting brackets
* ❋ Hammer and nails

1 Glue the pieces of wood together to form a zigzag pattern as shown in the photo. When the glue is dry, nail the pieces together.

2 Spread out your newspaper. Water down the coral paint (use two parts paint to one part water) and give the wood a wash of color.

3 When the paint has thoroughly dried, mount the rack on the wall with brackets in 3 different places. Add CDs and you're set!

Eye of God

What You'll Need:

* ❋ 2 30-inch long wooden dowels about ½ inch in diameter
* ❋ 1 skein each of 3 different colors of yarn (we used white, green, and beige)

1 Using your first color of yarn, tie the dowels together in the middle, forming a cross shape with the wood.

2 Starting in the center of the cross, loop the yarn around each stick, going from one stick to the next and switching colors every inch or so. Be sure to keep the wooden cross straight. To move from one yarn color to another, just tie off one color of yarn with a knot and tie on the new color, keeping all the knots on the back.

3 Tie a loop of yarn on the end of one dowel and hang with a nail.

Bean Box

What You'll Need:

✳ 1 bag each of dried red beans, green peas, yellow peas, and black beans

✳ 1 cigar box or other sturdy box

✳ Ribbon (we used 3 inches of brown)

✳ Clear-drying glue (like Elmer's)

✳ Pen or pencil

1 Draw a design on the box.

2 Apply glue to the box top and arrange the beans and peas on the wet glue. Let the box top dry overnight, then turn the box on its side and move on to the next surface. Leave the box on its side to dry, otherwise the beans and peas will fall off. Continue with one side up at a time until the box is covered with beans and peas and the design is complete. You can always make changes while the glue is still wet.

3 Make a bow with a piece of ribbon and glue to the top lid securely. This can be used as a handle.

Twig Magazine Rack

What You'll Need:

✳ About 10 willow branches (or whatever falls off the trees in your backyard or nearest park), cut to approximately equal length

✳ About 4 yards of twine

✳ Hammer and nails

✳ Scissors

1 Tie the tree branches together with twine about every 4 inches until you have a nice long row of them.

2 Attach to the wall with hammer and nails, and hang your magazines on them.

Bean Art

What You'll Need:

* 1 bag each of dried red beans, green peas, yellow peas, and black beans
* 1 piece of cardboard or an old picture frame
* Clear-drying glue (like Elmer's)
* Pen or pencil

1 Draw a design on the cardboard or old frame (attics, thrift shops, and garage sales are a great place to find these).

2 Fill in one area at a time with glue, placing the beans and peas on top of the glue.

3 Move to the next color until you're satisfied with your design. You can always make changes while the glue is still wet. Let it dry face up overnight, or the beans and peas will fall off.

Rope Wall Detail

What You'll Need:

* ½ gallon of flat-finish latex turquoise paint (see RESOURCES for details)
* Rope (roughly 15 feet, depending on your design)
* Paintbrush
* Newspaper
* Measuring tape
* Pencil
* Hammer and small nails

1 With a pencil, lightly draw an arch the size you would like it. We drew our arch 5 feet wide and 7 feet high. Round out the corners at the top to create your arch shape.

2 Lay out your newspaper, open a window, and paint the arch with the turquoise paint.

3 When the paint is dry, take the rope and nail it up on the wall with the small nails in a cool design inside the turquoise arch.

4 Erase the light pencil markings that formed the upper corners of your doorway.

Clay Pot Lamp

What You'll Need:

* 1 clay pot with a 1-inch hole in the bottom
* Turquoise and coral flat-finish latex paints (see RESOURCES for details)
* Light cord
* 15- to 25-watt bulb or lower
* Paintbrush
* Newspaper

1 Spread out some newspaper, and paint your pot with the paint colors used elsewhere in the room. (Make sure the pot has a hole in the bottom!)

2 String in a light cord. Using a 15- to 25-watt bulb, plug the pot in and you have a cool nightlight.

Wall Treatment

What You'll Need:

* 2 gallons of coral flat-finish latex paint (see RESOURCES for details)
* 1 gallon of turquoise paint (see RESOURCES for details)
* Paintbrushes or rollers
* Gloves
* Ladder
* Newspaper
* Measuring tape
* Pencil

1 Lay out your newspaper, open a window for ventilation. (You'll need to find somewhere else to sleep for the night.)

2 Paint the walls coral, leaving a 4-inch space around windows and doors.

3 Lightly draw a fake arch behind your bed, the more uneven the better—it makes it look natural, like the entrance to a real adobe house. (See Rope Wall Detail, page 61, for more information.)

4 When the coral paint has thoroughly dried, paint the edges around the windows and doors and the arch over the bed with the turquoise paint. Now you've captured the true essence of the Southwest.

Floral Headboard

What You'll Need:

❈ 1 piece of ¼-inch plywood, edges rounded, cut to fit your bed (a twin bed is 39-inches wide; a full is 54-inches wide; a queen is 60-inches wide)

❈ 2 pieces of pink satin, 2¼-yards long and 45-inches wide

❈ 1 piece of green satin, 2¼-yards long and 45-inches wide

❈ Plastic flowers and vines

❈ Staple gun

❈ Hammer and nails

1 Have the hardware store cut the plywood into a headboard to fit your bed. The person who cuts the wood for you should also be able to round it into a curved shape.

2 Staple the green satin to the bottom of the headboard, making little folds as you go to create a ruched, or pleated, effect. It will look somewhat like an open fan. Ultimately you want it to be 15-inches wide at the bottom and 25-inches wide at the top. Staple it into place. Be sure to overlap the fabric at the top of the wood. Use the pink pieces on either side of the green, covering the wood completely.

3 Staple the plastic flowers around the top of the headboard to cover its edges.

4 Nail the headboard to the wall to secure it, or try extra-strong double-stick tape. The weight of the bed will hold it in place.

Curtains

What You'll Need:

* 4 yards of light pink satin (45 inches wide) to make one curtain
* 4 yards of hot pink satin (45 inches wide) to make one curtain
* Sewing machine or needle and thread
* Plastic flowers
* Measuring tape
* Staple gun
* Scissors

1 Cut each piece of 4-yard-long fabric lengthwise, and sew the pieces together to create strips that are 8 yards long and approximately 22½ inches wide.

2 Stitch the two 8-yard-long pieces together lengthwise.

3 Finish the hems if you want to. (Most satin already has a nice edge but you might have to finish the hems at the bottom.)

4 Staple the curtains up by starting in the center, measuring as you go along to keep them even. Have a friend help you with the positioning.

5 Staple bunches of flowers wherever you like for even more flower-power punch.

Flower Lamp/Mirror/Picture Frame

What You'll Need:

* Lamp, mirror, and/or picture frame
* Plastic flowers
* Plastic bugs
* Glue gun
* Scissors

1 Snip the stems on the flowers to a ½ inch.

2 Use the glue gun to attach flowers and bugs in any way you like to whatever you like. Have fun!

Daisy Pillow

What You'll Need:

- ¼ yard of hot pink satin (45 inches wide)
- 2 yards of lavender satin (45 inches wide)
- 1 to 2 bags of pillow filling (or a cheap pillow from which you can remove the stuffing)
- Scissors
- Pencil
- Sewing machine or needle and thread

1 Cut 12 tear-shaped flower petals from the lavender satin; each should be about 12 inches long by 8 inches wide.

2 Sew the petals shiny-side in using a ½-inch seam allowance. Leave the hole toward the base of the petal. Turn right-side out and stuff the petals, closing up the ends and gathering them together at their smallest points to form the flower shape.

3 Fold the pink fabric in half and pin to hold it in place. Trace a circle 7 inches in diameter on one side to make the flower's center. Cut out the circle from the two layers of fabric at once so you'll have two circles the same size. Stitch them together inside out, leaving a small hole. Turn right-side out, stuff with filling, and sew petals closed.

Flower Pots

What You'll Need:

- Flower pots, any size or material (ours were terra-cotta but you can use any kind, including plastic)
- Latex or acrylic paint (we used light pink and red)
- Paintbrushes
- Newspaper

1 If necessary, wash pots thoroughly to remove any residual plant life or dirt. Let dry completely.

2 Lay out newspaper in your workspace. Paint the outside and inside of each pot with your choice of paint. Let dry.

3 Add polka dots in a contrasting color to the sides of the pot. You can also borrow a motif (flowers, bugs, or leaves) from other parts of the room and paint it on the pots instead.

Giant Tissue Paper Flowers

This is the material list for one flower.

What You'll Need:

❋ 8 standard sheets (30" x 20") of tissue paper (we used pink)

❋ Large rubber band

❋ 1 stick or dowel (Go to the park or your backyard for a stick—it's free!)

❋ Scissors

1 Fold all 8 sheets of tissue paper lengthwise every 2 inches, like an accordion. You will have a 20-inch-wide pleated piece of tissue paper.

2 Place the stick or dowel at the center of the strips of tissue paper. Wind the rubber band around the paper many times and secure it to the stick.

3 Take your scissors and round off the edges of the tissue paper to give the flower a scalloped appearance. Do only a bit at a time, as you can always cut more later.

4 Carefully peel the layers of tissue upward, starting from the top layer, which will become the middle of the flower. Continue all the way to the bottom sheets of paper, and arrange to your liking.

NOTE: You can change the color of your flowers with spray paint. Remember to lay down newspaper first and use a face mask.

satin pillows

This is the material list for one pillow.

What You'll Need:

❉ 1 yard of green satin (45 inches wide)

❉ 2 yards of pink satin (45 inches wide)

❉ 1 bag of pillow filling (or a cheap pillow from which you can remove the stuffing)

❉ Sewing machine or needle and thread

❉ Scissors

1 Cut the green satin into four matching leaves; each should be about 15 inches long by 10 inches wide.

2 Sew two leaves together inside out, allowing a ½-inch seam and leaving a 4-inch hole. Turn right-side out, stuff with pillow filling, and sew closed.

3 Cut the pink satin down the center lengthwise, creating two pieces of fabric 22½-inches wide and 2-yards long. Sew these two pieces together to create one piece 4-yards long and 22½-inches wide.

4 Fold the pink fabric in half lengthwise, shiny side out, and sew it into a long tube using ½-inch seam allowance. Stuff with pillow filling toward the center, about two yards, then twist the raw, unfinished edges in a circle so that they look like a whole rose, stitching the edges together as you go.

5 When you're down to the last yard, continue twisting and stitching, making sure that no raw edges show. Then attach the green fabric leaves to the undersides of the roses.

Wall Treatment

What You'll Need:

* 1 gallon each of lime green and pink flat-finish latex paint (see RESOURCES for details)
* Paintbrushes or rollers
* Gloves
* Newspaper
* Measuring tape
* Pencil
* Masking tape

1 Lay down newspaper and open a window for ventilation. (You'll need to find somewhere else to sleep for the night.)

2 Measure a line around the room 38 inches up from the floor and mark it with tape. Paint the wall below this point with lime green paint.

3 When the green coat is dry, remove the tape. Draw a line around the room with light pencil 36 inches up from the floor or 2 inches below the top of your green paint.

4 Carefully tape along your lightly drawn line. Now paint above it with the pink paint to the ceiling.

Resources for this Room

✳ ✳ ✳ ✳ ✳ ✳ ✳ ✳

PAINT: We used Benjamin Moore Key Lime 2031-50 flat-finish latex and Newborn Pink 2078-60 flat-finish latex.

FLOWERS and BUGS: We used plastic flower vines and plastic toy bugs from a 99-cent store (about $12 worth). You can also try craft stores and florist supply stores.

WOOD: We spent about $10 for basic plywood, cut at Home Depot.

FABRIC: We opted for an inexpensive satin fabric in various colors, about $4 per yard.

PILLOW FILLING: It's about $3 per bag and can be bought at most craft stores, or you can use an old pillow you already have around the house.

LAMP and MIRROR: Kmart has a nice range of sturdy lamps for $6 and up; mirrors start at around $5. You can also try flea markets, thrift stores, or garage sales, but be sure these older lamps are in good working order to avoid the possibility of fire. Older wood-backed mirrors tend to be much heavier than plastic ones; be careful how and where you hang them.

PICTURE FRAME: Ours came from Ikea, about $1. Try flea markets, thrift stores, or garage sales for slightly beat-up but usable frames.

DOUBLE-STICK TAPE: Pick this up at any hardware store for $1.

FLOWER POTS: Check out stores like Target or Kmart, where they go for about $2 each. You can also get them for free from the gardener in your family. And don't be shy about emptying out that half-dead plant.

CLEANING TIPS/HINTS: Spot clean the satin headboard, curtains, and pillows with Afta cleaning solution. If the plastic flowers on the frame, mirror, headboard and lamp begin to get dusty, try cleaning them with a Swiffer, which pulls the dust away from the flowers without knocking them off.

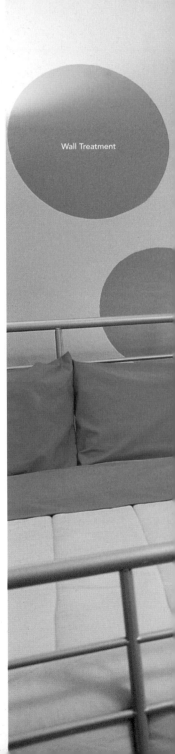

Chapter Nine

Morgan's ultra Mod

Wall Treatment

Morgan couldn't wait to get started on her room: before we arrived with our photographer, she had painted it blue! Because she has always been interested in design, Morgan was excited when we showed her the ultra-modern scheme for her room. She was thrilled with the final results: "I love my room! The orange gives it a lot of warmth, and the silver makes the room really vibrant. My friends all wanted to get theirs done, too." Her favorite part of the room is the lamp and she spends a lot of time at the desk, too. Math is Morgan's best subject in school. After school, she likes to surf the net, shop, and hang out with friends. Though she still loves design, she thinks she'll choose a career in finance.

Light Reflection Window Hanging

Plastic Cup Ball

Silver Lamp

Beaded Frame

Bean-Shaped
Table

Beaded Frame

What You'll Need:

* 1 frame
* Strands of fake plastic pearls or beads, any color
* Spray paint, silver (see RESOURCES for details)
* Newspaper
* Glue gun
* Face mask

1 Hot glue the rope(s) of pearls or beads from the inside edge of the frame outward, working your way out one row at a time until you reach the outer edge of the frame.

2 When the glue dries, lay down your newspaper, put on your face mask, and spray paint the whole thing silver. (Be sure to work in a well-ventilated area, and hold the can 8 inches from the frame's surface. Shake the can each time you spray.)

3 Let dry completely. Add a photo or other image.

Light-Reflection Window Hanging

What You'll Need:

* About 30 foil-backed lids (from takeout food containers—see RESOURCES for details)
* 1 box of small, silver paperclips
* Silver-toned curtain rod
* Hole puncher

1 Punch holes at the top and bottom of each takeout lid.

2 Connect the lids with paperclips, using 3 clips in between each disk.

3 After making a row of 6, attach it to your curtain rod with another paper-clip. Hang as many rows as you want for your desired effect. It's great when they catch the light and shine it into the room. You can also hang these with cool shower-curtain rings!

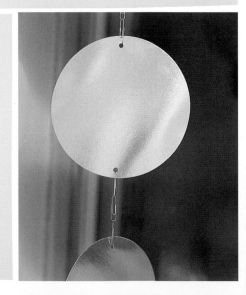

Plastic-Cup Ball

This is strictly decorative: it's not a lamp, but it still looks really cool hanging in your room, and it's fun to make.

What You'll Need:

❊ 250 plastic cups (we used blue)

❊ Thin chain or heavy ribbon (length depends on your ceiling height and how low you want the ball to hang)

❊ Ceiling hook

❊ Spray paint, optional (we used silver—see RESOURCES for details)

❊ Newspaper

❊ Glue gun

❊ Face mask

1 Hot glue the cups together at their rims and bases. Keep adding the cups until you start to see the ball forming. Trust us, it will. (This took a good hour to finish, even with the help of a friend!)

2 Just for fun, we took some silver spray paint and dusted the edges of the cups for a cooler effect. Remember to lay out newspaper in a well-ventilated area and to wear your face mask. (Be sure to shake the can each time you spray and keep the can 8 inches away from the ball's surface.)

3 Once the paint is thoroughly dry, hot glue your chain or ribbon to the ball so you can hang it.

4 Put a hook in the ceiling, and hang at the desired height.

Silver Lamp

What You'll Need:

* 1 lamp
* About 20 feet of plastic beads (try Christmas beads)
* Spray paint, silver (see RESOURCES for details)
* Silver-topped light bulb
* Silver duct tape (optional)
* Newspaper
* Glue gun
* Face mask

1 Remove the lampshade from the lamp and the fabric from the shade. Cover any sharp edges of the metal or wire frame of the shade (where your hand would get scratched when changing bulbs or turning the lamp on and off) with silver duct tape.

2 Hot glue 6-inch, 7-inch and 8-inch strips of beads to the top wire every ½ inch all of the way around until the beads hang all of the way around and create the shade.

3 Lay down your newspaper, put on your face mask, and spray paint the lamp base. (Be sure to work in a well-ventilated area, shaking the can each time you spray and keeping the can 8 inches from the lamp's surface.)

4 Use a light bulb with a silver top so the light won't be too harsh. Add your beaded shade and you're done.

Wall Treatment

What You'll Need:

* 2 gallons of flat-finish latex paint (we used blue— see RESOURCES for details)
* 1 quart of flat-finish latex paint in a contrasting color (we used orange—see RESOURCES for details)
* Paintbrush and roller

* Ladder
* Gloves
* Pieces of string of varying lengths
* Newspaper
* Pencil
* Tack

1 Lay down your newspaper and open a window. (You'll need to find somewhere else to sleep for the night.)

2 Paint the walls blue (or whatever color you've decided on). Let dry.

3 Tack the string on the wall in the middle of where you want to place a circle. Tie a pencil to the end of the string, and keeping the string taut at all times, lightly draw a circle. Repeat in as many different spots as you like. You can vary the size of the circle by changing the length of your string.

4 Paint the circles with the contrasting color.

Bean-Shaped Table

This takes some work, but it's worth it!

What You'll Need:

* ½ a sheet of ½-inch-thick plywood
* 4 metal L brackets (2 for each leg)
* 16 ½-inch screws
* 1 quart of high-gloss latex paint
  (we used blue—see RESOURCES for details)
* 1 can of spray paint (we used orange—
  see RESOURCES for details)
* 1 place mat with a cut-out design to use as a
  stencil (you can create a stencil yourself, too)
* Paintbrush
* Newspaper
* Wood glue
* Sandpaper
* Saw
* Screwdriver
* Pencil
* Face mask

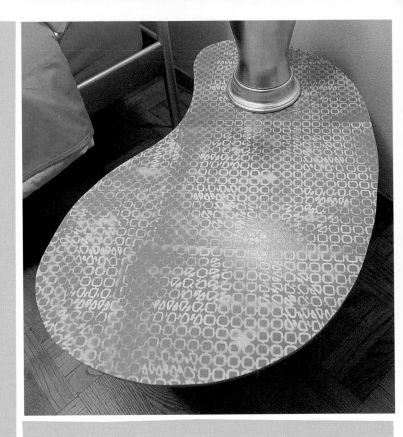

1 Trace a bean shape on your plywood by drawing
   an oval shape 3 feet long and 2 feet wide with one
   side of the oval curving 6 inches toward the middle
   and cut it out with the saw. Cut out two square
   pieces of plywood between 12 and 16 inches high
   for the legs. (Or trace the shape on the wood and
   have a hardware store cut it out for you.)

2 Once you have all your pieces cut, sand the rough edges
   and attach the legs with the L brackets, which is easy to
   do with a screwdriver and screws. Make sure you spread
   glue on the wood before you screw on the legs to make it
   even sturdier.

3 When the glue is thoroughly dry, lay out your newspaper,
   turn the table upright, and paint it blue.

4 The last step is to take your table on your newspaper to a
   well-ventilated area, put on a face mask, lay your cut-out
   place mat over the top of the table, and spray paint it
   orange. (Be sure to shake the can each time you spray and
   keep the can 8 inches away from the table's surface.) Wait
   for the paint to dry, put on your stuff and you're done.

Other Cool Stuff

We picked up dark blue and white mini-rugs and made one big rug by taping them together on the bottom with heavy-duty duct tape.

We also spray-painted Morgan's desk with silver radiator spray paint; we chose silver because it is one of her favorite colors. Be sure to work in a well-ventilated area if you decide to do this.

Resources for this Room

❈ ❈ ❈ ❈ ❈ ❈ ❈ ❈

PAINT: Benjamin Moore Little Boy Blue 2061-60 flat-finish latex and Benjamin Moore Citrus Blast 2018-30 flat-finish latex (for the circles). Krylon chrome (silver) spray paint for the lamp and Krylon orange for the table, $3 for each can.

PLASTIC PEARLS: Pick them up cheap at a 99-cent store or a craft store like Treasure Island. You can also use Christmas tree garlands.

LAMP: This was an old lamp we found it at a secondhand store: a steal at $3. Its lampshade was broken, but that was fine because we were going to change the shade covering. Try flea markets, thrift stores, or garage sales, but be sure these older lamps are in good working order to avoid the possibility of fire.

DESK and CHAIR: We used an old desk of Morgan's. Ikea also has great, inexpensive furniture; that's where we picked up her desk chair (about $28).

SILVER TAKEOUT LIDS: If nobody cooks at your house, these should accumulate pretty fast. If not, check out 99-cent stores or Job Lot stores, where they are 3 for $1.

PLASTIC CUPS and PICTURE FRAME: From the 99-cent store, too—our decorating mecca.

CARPETS: These remnants were $1.99 each at a carpet store. You can also try Home Depot or Kmart.

SILVER-TOPPED LIGHTBULB: Any hardware store stocks these; about $2 each.

Chapter Ten

Heather and Crystal's at the Bazaar

These twins share one small room in a city apartment, so you know it has to look extra spiffy. Both girls love their new, eye-catching space, which Crystal and her friends call "the inside of (I Dream of) Jeannie's bottle!" Heather says, "Because we love it so much, we really try to keep it looking as clean as we can." Heather, right, is a vintage-clothes-loving artist who plans to continue her art studies at college. Crystal, left, likes working with kids and hanging out with friends. She is studying government in school and wants to be a teacher one day.

Wall Treatment

Curtains

Lamp

Popsicle Stick Mirror

Pillows

Comforter Cover

Small Purple Table

Curtains

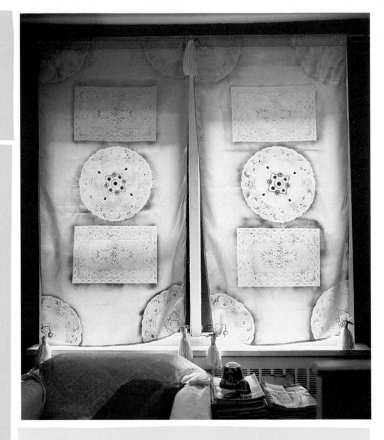

What You'll Need:

- Satin (we used 3 yards—measure your windows to determine how much you'll need)
- Spray paint (we used gold and hot pink—see RESOURCES for details)
- Plastic lace place mat or about 1 yard of real lace (it's the pattern you're after here, not the quality, so polyester is fine)
- Plastic jewels
- Yarn to make your own tassels (see below)
- Glitter glue
- Glue gun
- Staple gun
- Newspaper
- Sewing machine or needle and thread
- Face mask
- Ladder

1 Cut and finish the ends of the satin fabric to make curtains to match the size of your windows. Measure your windows to determine how much fabric you'll need. This window treatment called for two panels that were 20 inches wide and 60 inches long.

2 Finish the edges by folding over the raw edges of the fabric to create a ½-inch hem on the bottom and sides of the curtain. At the top, fold the fabric over 1½ inches to create a sleeve for your curtain rod. Straight stitch them using your sewing machine or hand sew them with ½-inch stitches.

3 Lay out your newspaper in a well-ventilated area. Place the satin flat on top of it and lay the plastic lace place mat or the lace fabric on top of the satin. Put on your face mask, and use the spray paint to create a lace pattern, letting the paint dry between colors. (Be sure to shake the can well each time you spray, and keep the can about 8 inches from the surface you're spraying.)

4 When the paint is dry, attach the plastic jewels with your glitter glue to the center of the spray painted lace.

5 Hang the curtains using the staple gun and sew on the tassels. (To make your own, follow the directions on page 29.)

Popsicle Stick Mirror

What You'll Need:

- 8" x 8" mirror tile
- 8" x 8" cardboard
- Popsicle sticks
- Glitter (we used gold)
- Ribbon or string
- Mounting screw
- Acrylic paint (we used purple)
- Paintbrush
- Glue gun or other strong glue that will adhere to glass

1 In a well-ventilated area, paint the Popsicle sticks your desired color, and while the paint is still wet, sprinkle glitter around the sticks' edges. Let dry.

2 Glue the Popsicle sticks onto the mirror in the design of your choice.

3 Use the glue gun to attach the cardboard to the back of the mirror, then attach a ribbon or string to the back to hang.

4 Let dry overnight and hang on the wall with the mounting screw. (Note: If you hang the mirror near a light source it will brighten your room.)

Comforter Cover

What You'll Need:

- 2 twin-size flat sheets
- About a yard of ribbon
- Spray paint (we used gold and hot pink—see RESOURCES for details)
- Plastic lace place mat or about 1 yard of real lace (it's the pattern you're after here, not the quality, so polyester is fine)
- Newspaper
- Sewing machine or needle and thread
- Face mask
- Scissors

1 Sew the two sheets together, leaving the top (horizontal) end open like a big pillow case.

2 Sew ribbons on either side of the opening every 15 inches. The ribbons should be opposite each other so that you can tie them together once the comforter is inside the cover.

3 Lay out your newspaper, place the plastic lace place mats or lace fabric on the sheets, put on your face mask, and spray paint a design. (Be sure to shake the can well each time you spray, and keep the can about 8 inches from the surface you're spraying.) Move the placemat or lace fabric ¼-inch and use your contrasting spray paint color. Repeat this until you have a pattern you like.

Lamp

What You'll Need:

- 1 lamp
- Spray paint (we used orange for the base and gold for the pattern—see RESOURCES for details)
- Plastic lace place mat or about 1 yard of real lace (it's the pattern you're after here, not the quality, so polyester is fine)
- 1 yard of hot pink satin (22½ inches wide)
- 2 yards of trim or ribbon
- Newspaper
- Glue gun
- Face mask
- Pencil

1 Remove the lampshade from your lamp. Spread out your newspaper in a well-ventilated area, put on your face mask, and spray the base of your lamp with your chosen color. (Be sure to shake the can well each time you spray, and keep the can about 8 inches from the surface you're spraying.) Let it dry thoroughly.

2 Cover the base with the plastic lace place mat or lace fabric and spray paint it with the contrasting color to stencil on the lace pattern. Don't worry about perfection; it will look cool even if the patterns don't completely match.

3 Make a pattern for the lampshade by first tracing and then cutting out six sections of satin. Hot glue them over the old lampshade fabric. Hot glue pieces of trim or ribbon over the edges.

Small Purple Table

What You'll Need:

- 1 table
- Plastic lace place mat or about 1 yard of lace (it's the pattern you're after here, not the quality, so polyester is fine)
- Spray paint (we used purple for the base and gold for the pattern—see RESOURCES for details)
- Newspaper
- Face mask
- Sandpaper

1 Prep your table by making sure it is clear of any residue or dirt and completely dry. You might want to scratch it up with some sandpaper to create a porous surface.

2 Spread out your newspaper in a well-ventilated area, put on your face mask, and spray paint the table purple, taking care to leave no bare spots. (Be sure to shake the can well each time you spray, and keep the can about 8 inches from the surface you're spraying.)

3 After the paint is thoroughly dry, lay the place mat or fabric lace over the tabletop and spray paint it gold (or the second color of your choice) to create a lace pattern.

4 Let dry completely.

Pillows

What You'll Need to Make One Pillow:

- 1 standard pillowcase (to use as a pattern) and pillow
- ½ yard each of hot pink and light pink satin
- Plastic lace place mat or about 1 yard of real lace (it's the pattern you're after here, not the quality of the lace, so polyester will do fine)
- Pillow
- Spray paint (we used gold—see RESOURCES for details)
- Plastic jewels
- Yarn to make your own tassels (see page 29 for instructions)
- Measuring tape
- Newspaper
- Glitter glue
- Sewing machine or needle and thread
- Scissors
- Face mask
- Pencil

1 Measure the dimensions of one side of a standard pillow. Add 1 inch all around to allow for a seam. Cut the pattern out of the hot pink and light pink satin. You are creating a new pillowcase of satin with hot pink on one side and light pink on the other.

2 Sew the satin pieces together, inside out, allowing a ½-inch seam and leaving one end open. Turn right-side out.

3 Lay out your newspaper in a well-ventilated area, put on your face mask, and place the satin flat on top of the newspaper. Layer the plastic lace place mat or fabric on top. Spray paint the lace to create a pattern.

4 When the paint is dry, use the glitter glue to add the plastic jewels in a pattern you like in the center of the spray-painted lace design.

5 Use the instructions on page 29 to create tassels. Sew them to the corners of your case. Add a pillow and you're done!

Wall Treatment

What You'll Need:

- **1 gallon each of light pink, hot pink, and orange flat-finish latex paint (see RESOURCES for details)**
- **Paintbrush and roller**
- **Gloves**
- **Newspaper**
- **Ladder**

1 Lay down your newspaper, open a window, and find somewhere else to sleep for the night!

2 Paint two walls opposite each other light pink. Paint another wall hot pink, and the remaining wall orange.

Resources for this Room

❋ ❋ ❋ ❋ ❋ ❋ ❋ ❋

PAINT: We used three different Benjamin Moore colors for the walls: one gallon of Tangelo 2017-30 flat-finish latex, one gallon of Hot Lips 2077-30 flat-finish latex, and one gallon of Light Chiffon Pink 2000-60 flat-finish latex. We also used Krylon spray paint in purple, hot pink, gold, and orange; cans are about $3 each.

COMFORTER and PILLOWS: We picked up some inexpensive twin-size white flat sheets and pillowcases at Target.

MIRROR: An 8" x 8" mirror tile costs about $3 at just about any hardware store.

TABLE: Try flea markets, thrift stores, or garage sales for slightly beat-up but usable tables.

POPSICLE STICKS: You can pick them up at a craft supply store for 99 cents.

LAMP: The one we used cost $10. Try Kmart, which has a nice range of sturdy lamps for $6 and up; mirrors start at around $5. Or you can try flea markets, thrift stores, or garage sales, but be sure these older lamps are in good working order to avoid the possibility of fire.

PLASTIC LACE PLACE MATS: We picked these up at a 99-cent store. We recommend buying a few for this room as the spray paint begins to accumulate after a few uses.

GLITTER GLUE, YARN FOR TASSELS, and PLASTIC JEWELS: Check out Michael's craft supply stores, where plastic jewels are about $1 per packet. Glitter glue is about $1.50.

CLEANING TIPS/HINTS: If the pillowcases and comforter cover get dirty, gently wash them by hand with some Woolite and allow to air dry. They'll last longer that way. We recommend the Swiffer for cleaning anything with jewels and glitter on it, like the mirror. It pulls away the dust but leaves the sparkle behind.

Chapter Eleven

Jenny's Asian Medley

Ladder Shelf

Jenny likes Asian style, so this theme was a natural for her. "I love having friends over and hanging out in my room!" It turns out that this pretty room is as practical as it is decorative: "The shelves and the chair are my favorite parts. I love sitting at the chair. I used to have a crate for all my stuff, and the shelves work so much better. And the blue walls are very soothing." Her parents really like it, too. Jenny's best subjects are English, art and math, and she wants to study photography next year. After school she works part-time as a student teacher, helping first graders with homework and art. She'd like to be a writer, teacher, or chef.

Wall Stencil

Red Chair

Decoupage Candles

What You'll Need:

* 2 glass candle holders
* 2 candles
* Asian-language newspaper, origami paper, or other thin Asian-inspired paper
* Clear-drying glue (like Elmer's)
* Scissors

1 Cut your chosen paper into pieces that are roughly 2" x 2".

2 Cover the outside of the glass with glue, paste on the paper, then paint over the paper with more glue. Keep doing this until you have covered the entire outside of the glass.

Chopstick Frame

What You'll Need:

* About 20 chopsticks
* Clear-drying glue (like Elmer's)
* Tape

1 Place five chopsticks in a row and glue them together until you have 4 sets of 5 chopsticks.

2 Crisscross the sets as shown, left, and glue them together.

3 Tape a photo or other image in the back.

HINT: We used chopsticks with a permanent stained finish, but if the chopsticks you use are the plain wood variety, you might want to paint them.

Ladder Shelf

What You'll Need:

* 2 pieces of 5' x 6" x 1" pine board
* 5 pieces of 12" x 6" x 1" pine board
* 1 quart of high-gloss red paint (see RESOURCES for details)
* Pencil
* Paintbrush
* Gloves
* Newspaper
* Measuring tape
* Wood glue
* Hammer and nails
* Face mask

1 Decide how far apart you would like to space your shelves and with a pencil, mark their placement on one of the 5-foot-long pieces of wood. Place some wood glue on the short edge of a 12-inch piece, place it on the long piece of wood where you've marked your first shelf, and nail the pieces together, hitting the nail through the long piece of wood on the opposite side from where the glue is. Repeat with the other 12-inch pieces, then glue their other sides, lay on the other 5-foot piece of wood, and nail together. Let the glue dry.

2 Spread newspaper in a well-ventilated area, put on your face mask and gloves, and paint your shelf.

When your shelf is thoroughly dry, put your CDs and cool knickknacks on it.

Red Chair

What You'll Need:

❋ 1 chair with upholstered seat or separate cushion

❋ 1 yard of fabric (we used pink polyester satin)

❋ 2 yards of fringe (we used orange)

❋ 1 quart of high-gloss paint (we used red—
see RESOURCES for details)

❋ Paintbrush

❋ Newspaper

❋ Gloves

❋ Staple gun

❋ Glue gun

1 Remove the seat from the chair. Save any nails or screws so you can reattach it later. Lay out your newspaper in a well-ventilated area, put on your gloves, and paint the chair red. Let dry completely.

2 Re-cover the seat with a vivid fabric of your choice. (We went with pink because, combined with the red, it's really eye-popping, but light blue or black would also look beautiful.) Stretch the new fabric right over the old fabric and staple in place on the underside of the seat. Screw the seat back on and hot glue some trim to the edge of the cushion. (We used orange to add even more contrast.)

HINT: Use a durable fabric that can be spot cleaned (pen marks, food stains—hey, we know . . .) and that will wear well with use (e.g., chair as step stool, not to mention continual hiney action!). But don't opt out on the glamour factor! If need be, you can always replace it with another yard of fabric.

Chinese-Laundry Photo Album

This couldn't be easier!

What You'll Need:

❋ 4 1-yard-long pieces of colored twine (we used blue)

❋ About 20 plastic multicolored clothes pins

❋ Small Chinese lanterns (optional)

❋ Thumbtacks

1 Push the thumbtacks into the back of a door, a wall, or a corkboard.

2 String twine between them and hang your favorite things with the clothes pins. Accentuate with the lanterns if you wish.

You can hang postcards and photos, necklaces, mementos—whatever you want.

Wall Stencil

What You'll Need:

* 1 large paper bag
* 1 quart of flat-finish paint (we used red—see RESOURCES for details)
* Paintbrush
* Newspaper
* Pencil
* Light tape
* Scissors

1 Cut open the large paper bag to make a piece of paper big enough for the stencil.

2 Fold the paper in half to create the double image and draw a pointy design like the one in the photo. You could also refer to an Asian art or architecture book for ideas, or just use your imagination.

3 Cut out your stencil and unfold it. Tape it to the wall and lightly trace the pattern onto the wall.

4 Spread out your newspaper and paint in the stencil with the red paint. Use a small paintbrush on the edges to get your lines really neat.

Other Cool Stuff

Hook 3 round paper lanterns together and hang them over the bed. We used white, but you can use any color or combination of colors (pulling in the pink from the chair seat would look really nice).

We picked up some unused food containers to create organizers. These are great for nail polish, makeup, hair accessories, pens and pencils—you name it. You can even decorate them with paint pens or Magic Markers.

The pillows and curtains are made from a fabric that looked Asian to us. We accessorized the room with an inexpensive grass mat and woven baskets. We used bamboo place mats on the shelves and some cool black polished stones to give a Zen feel. We hung a matchstick blind on the wall and inexpensive Chinese paper fans on the walls. We also threw in a basket with a lid to keep dirty clothes off the floor (thought you were the only one who does that?)!

Resources for this Room

✳ ✳ ✳ ✳ ✳ ✳ ✳ ✳

PAINT: We used Benjamin Moore Bonfire 2001-20 and Benjamin Moore Bluebelle 2064-70 in high-gloss and flat-finish latex.

CHAIR: We found this one at the flea market for about $10. Keep your eyes open—you'll find the perfect one.

FABRIC: We used one yard of hot pink Chinese brocade that was about $15 per yard.

GRASS MAT: These grass mats can be found online at www.pearlriver.com.

BASKETS: These are from Pier 1, about $14 each.

CANDLES: Many supermarkets sell them and so do 99-cent stores for about $1 each.

MATCHSTICK BLIND: Ours cost about $14 at Pier 1.

LANTERNS and PAPER FANS: They cost about $2 each and can be found at Asian markets. Or try the Oriental Trading Company (call for a catalog):1-800-228-2269 or online: www.orientaltrading.com.

CHOPSTICKS: Get them at an Asian takeout restaurant or grab some cool lacquered ones at an Asian market.

PAPER FOOD CONTAINERS: Ask at a Chinese or other Asian restaurant for some containers (free!), or pick some up at an Asian grocery store or restaurant supply store (about $5). Cool plastic ones are available online at www.containerstore.com.

CLEANING TIP/HINT: Clean the candles, frames, and wall hanging with a Swiffer, which will pull away the dust without damaging your decorations.

Chapter Twelve

Talia's african safari

"Totally relaxing" is how Talia describes her cool new suite: "At night I see the green, and I fall right asleep." Her new décor has also inspired her to begin a collection of African knickknacks: "I've been adding things to the shelf Mark made me, collecting wooden elephants and other African things." She told us it's a lot easier for her to settle down to her studies in her soothing room. There's only one downside to having such a comfortable, fun living space: "My friends never leave my room! It's like a little apartment of my own." Talia is a cheerleader who attends interschool cheering competitions, and her favorite things to do (after homework's done) are hanging out with friends and going to movies. Math is her favorite subject. She wants to be a criminal lawyer, and she's already pursuing this interest with an internship at the local DA's office.

Twine Frame

Drawer Shelf

Painted Mirror

Palm Leaf Stencil

Pencil Cup

Faux Fur Rug

Painted Mirror

What You'll Need:

* ❋ 1 wardrobe mirror
* ❋ 1 quart of high-gloss enamel paint (we used brown—see **RESOURCES** for details)
* ❋ Paintbrush
* ❋ Gloves
* ❋ Newspaper
* ❋ Masking tape (½-inch thick)

1 Lay out your newspaper, put on your gloves, and paint different designs on the mirror, leaving about a ½-inch of space between each painted shape. (We chose a random abstract design, but you can paint uneven stripes or squares, too. To make it easier, mark off areas with the masking tape and paint between the tape.) Remember, this paint is sticky; for clean up, use mineral oil on your brushes and nail-polish remover on your hands.

NOTE: You can also use a palm leaf stencil (see page 100) directly on the mirror or on the side of a drawer (see page 101). Remember, when something is inexpensive, you can experiment as much as you want. You have nothing to lose, and you just may come up with the next cool piece of super suite décor!

Pencil Cup

What You'll Need:

* 1 one-liter plastic soda bottle or soup can
* 1 ball of twine
* Clear-drying glue (like Elmer's)
* Scissors
* Masking tape

1 If you are using a plastic bottle, cut off the top. Tape over any sharp edges.

2 Glue one end of twine to the top of the bottle/can, and start wrapping it around the bottle, gluing down the twine as you go along.

3 When you get to the bottom, glue down the end, and tape it with some masking tape so it doesn't slip. Let it dry. You can make this cup a bit higher for flowers or lower for small clutter on your dresser.

Twine Frame

What You'll Need:

* 1 large piece of cardboard
* 1 ball of twine
* Measuring tape
* Tack or double-stick tape
* Clear-drying glue (like Elmer's)
* Scissors

1 Cut out the shape of frame that you'd like from the cardboard (ours is about 6" by 10").

2 Measure the photo or other image you want to frame. Cut a hole in the center of your frame that is a bit smaller than the image.

3 Working from the inside out, cover part of the frame with glue, and add twine in pieces or one long strip. Continue until the whole frame is covered.

4 When the glue is dry, tape your photo to the back and hang it on your wall with a small tack or some double-stick tape.

Palm Leaf Stencil (on walls)

What You'll Need:
- ☀ **Several palm leaves**
- ☀ **1 gallon flat-finish latex paint (we used green—see RESOURCES for details)**
- ☀ **Spray paint (we used dark brown, see RESOURCES for details)**
- ☀ **Paintbrush and roller**
- ☀ **Gloves**
- ☀ **Newspapers**
- ☀ **Face mask**
- ☀ **Masking tape**

1 Open the windows of your room, lay down some newspaper, and find somewhere else to sleep for the night.

2 Paint all the walls green. Let dry.

3 Tape the palm leaves by their stems to the walls. Put on your face mask and gloves and lightly spray paint over them. This leaves an impression of a leaf on the wall. (Be sure to shake the can each time you spray and hold the can 8 inches from the wall's surface.)

4 Continue around the room until you get the effect you want. You may want to do this halfway up the wall, all the way around the room—it looks really cool.

Drawer Shelf

A recycled dresser drawer makes a great shelf for displaying pictures, knickknacks, or CDs.

What You'll Need:
- ☀ 1 dresser drawer
- ☀ 1 yard of fabric
- ☀ 1 piece of cardboard (sized to fit the bottom of your drawer)
- ☀ Spray paint (we used dark brown— see RESOURCES for details)
- ☀ Newspaper
- ☀ Glue gun
- ☀ Measuring tape
- ☀ Strong tape, like packing tape
- ☀ Face mask
- ☀ Nails or screws

1 Lay out your newspaper in a well-ventilated area, put on your face mask, and spray paint the drawer. (Be sure to shake the can well each time you spray and hold the can at least 8 inches from the surface you're working on.)

2 While the paint is drying, cover your piece of cardboard with fabric, taping the fabric to the back of the cardboard so no one can see it.

3 When the paint is thoroughly dry, glue your fabric-covered cardboard into the inside bottom of the drawer.

4 Nail or screw the drawer to the wall as pictured, right.

HINT: You can also use a palm leaf stencil (see the previous project) on the drawer to create visual interest.

Faux Fur Rug and Pillow

What You'll Need:

* 1½ yards of faux fur (for the rug)
* 1 yard of faux fur (for the pillow)
* 1 bag of pillow stuffing (or a cheap pillow from which you can remove the stuffing)
* Rubber backing (optional)
* Magitak glue (optional)
* 1 package of double-stick tape
* Scissors

1 Cut your faux fur into a bone shape. No need to finish off the edges.

2 Use double-stick tape to secure the rug to the floor so it won't move around. (You can also add rubber backing, which can be easily applied with Magitak fabric glue.)

3 For the pillow, cut the fabric into two pieces of the same size; we chose 16" x 20" rectangles.

4 Sew the pieces together inside out, allowing a ½-inch seam and a 4-inch hole for stuffing. Turn right-side out, stuff, and sew up the hole.

Other Cool Stuff

We tacked inexpensive gauze above the window and tied it with raffia, which you can get at any craft store.

We gave plants a more prominent place in the room to create a jungle feel.

We stenciled the base of an old flea market lamp with our Palm Leaf Stencil. We then covered the lampshade with a piece of brown fabric to match the room.

We had a small garden fence left over from another room and decided to put it in the window to make the room earthier.

The beautiful bamboo print of the comforter brings the whole room together.

Resources for this Room

✳ ✳ ✳ ✳ ✳ ✳ ✳ ✳

PAINT: We used Benjamin Moore Stem Green 2029-40 flat-finish latex for the walls. For the stencil, we used dark brown spray paint from Krylon, $3 for each can. For the mirror, we used Benjamin Moore Rich Clay Brown 2164-30 in high-gloss enamel.

COMFORTER: This bamboo-print comforter was found at Linens N Things, $45.

WARDROBE MIRROR: Ours came from Kmart, about $7.99.

DRESSER: In New York City, people put their unwanted furniture out on the street, so it's an ongoing free flea market. We found an old dresser on the street and dragged a drawer home. (Of course, we cleaned it really well!) Look in thrift shops and flea markets, or in the attic.

DOUBLE-STICK TAPE (or Magitak fabric glue): You can get this at any fabric store or in the crafts department at Wal-Mart, about $3.

TWINE: We got this twine at a 99-cent store. Sometimes it comes in different colors, so keep an eye out for them. Variety is the spice of life!

PALM LEAVES: Floridians and Californians: Tell your younger sibling you'll give him or her a quarter for every palm tree leaf he or she can find. If you don't live in a tropical or semitropical area, go to any good florist, where you can pick them up for about a buck each.

Chapter Thirteen

Ria's Industrial Design

Cookie Sheet Headboard

This room is about rethinking everyday objects. Ria was amazed to see ordinary kitchen products adorning her bedroom. "The mood is so modern and new. It used to be so boring!" Her favorite parts of the room are the lamp, which she says is "really cool and sturdy," and the CD jewel-box picture holders. For part-time work, Ria helps out at a grade school. She takes a lot of writing and art classes, writes in her spare time, and plans to study liberal arts one day.

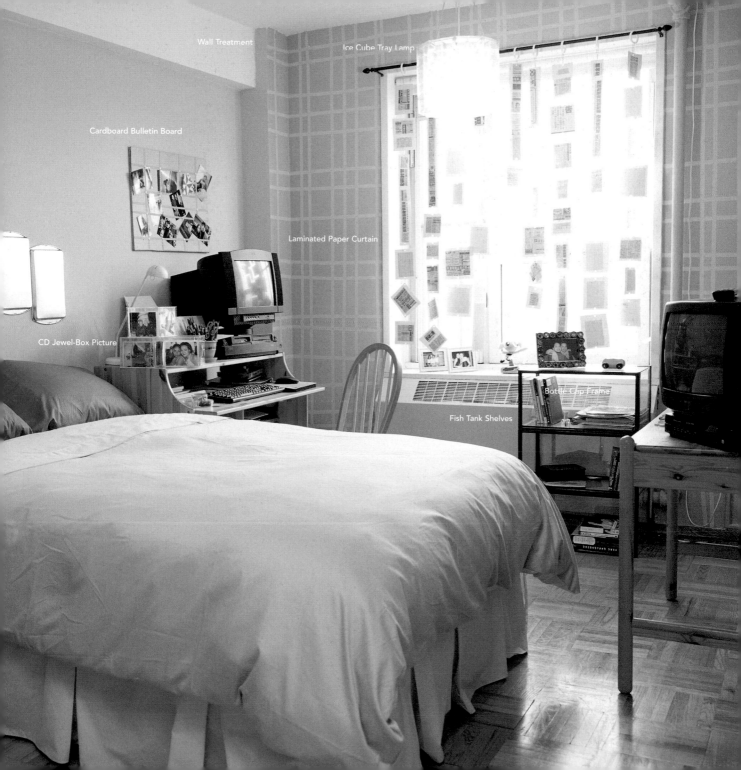

Wall Treatment

Ice Cube Tray Lamp

Cardboard Bulletin Board

Laminated Paper Curtain

CD Jewel-Box Picture

Bottle Cap Frame

Fish Tank Shelves

Laminated Paper Curtain

Paper is one of the best and cheapest ways to decorate! We used a Chinese-language newspaper. But this project can be done in a hundred ways, with photos of friends, different colors of paper, etc.

What You'll Need:
* ❄ Cool-looking paper
* ❄ 1 roll clear Con–Tact paper
* ❄ Manila folders
* ❄ Paper clips
* ❄ Shower curtain rings
* ❄ Hole puncher
* ❄ Scissors

1 Cut out squares of paper of various sizes and laminate them onto manila folders with clear Con–Tact paper.

2 Cut out shapes from the laminated paper and punch holes on the top and bottom. Connect them with paper clips. Use shower curtain rings to hang them up from a curtain rod, or anywhere else you like.

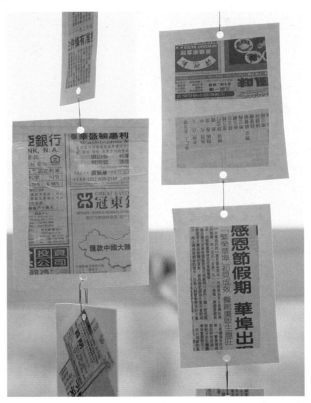

Bottle Cap Frame

What You'll Need:

* 20 bottle caps
* 1 picture frame
* Spray paint (we used dark blue—see RESOURCES for details)
* Glitter
* Shoe-box lid
* Newspaper
* Glue gun
* Plastic rhinestones or jewels
* Face mask

1 Glue your bottle caps to an old frame.

2 Lay down your newspaper, put on your face mask, and spray paint the frame. (Be sure to work in a well-ventilated area, shake the can each time you spray, and keep the can 8 inches from the surface you're spraying.)

3 While the paint is still wet, put the frame in the lid of a shoe box (trust us—you want to avoid making a mess with this stuff), and sprinkle tons of glitter over the whole thing.

4 When the frame is thoroughly dry, hot glue rhinestones into the center of each bottle cap.

This frame deserves a really special photo!

Cardboard Bulletin Board

What You'll Need:

* 2 18" x 24" pieces of cardboard
* 1 yard of fabric (we used gray)
* Ribbon
* Masking tape
* Thumbtacks

This is the easiest! Tape the pieces of cardboard together. Stretch the fabric over the cardboard and tape it to the back. Attach the ribbon with thumbtacks.

CD Jewel-box Picture

What You'll Need:

❋ Lots of CD jewel cases (we used a mix of light colors and clear—see RESOURCES for details)

❋ Glue gun

1 Snap out the plastic center that holds the CD. There will now be a slot on the side through which you can slip your photo.

2 Hot glue the cases together on the sides to form a box, using very thin strips of glue. Important: make sure the slot side is on the outside.

Make several boxes and stack them up for a tower of pictures.

Cookie Sheet Headboard

What You'll Need:

❋ 6 small cookie sheets (when shopping, bring along a magnet to make sure the sheets are magnetic—aluminum won't work)

❋ Magnets

❋ Hammer and nails

1 Using a large nail, hammer holes in the tops and bottoms of your cookie sheets.

2 Using the holes, nail the sheets to the wall over the head of the bed in a jagged pattern. Use magnets to add photos, pictures, notes—whatever you want. It's a great place to put things you've got to see first thing in the morning!

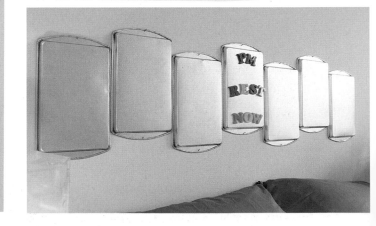

Ice Cube Tray Lamp

What You'll Need:

✳ 9 ice cube trays (we used light blue)

✳ ½ yard of ribbon (we used blue)

✳ 1 light cord/fixture

✳ 25-watt bulb or lower

✳ Ceiling hook

✳ Glue gun

1 Glue the sides of your trays together with hot glue so they form a circle as pictured, right.

2 Hot glue the ribbon to 3 different places on the structure. We did this between every 3 trays so it was even. Tie the tops of the ribbons together.

3 Hang the lamp from a ceiling hook and thread the light cord through as pictured, right.

NOTE: Use no higher than a 25-watt bulb.

Fish Tank Shelves

What You'll Need:

- 3 10-gallon fish tanks
- Glue gun

1 Clean your fish tanks thoroughly, using Windex or some other type of glass cleaner.

2 Stack one tank on top of the other, using a bit of glue between the edges to make it sturdy. You can also vary the size of the tanks you use.

Wall Treatment

What You'll Need:

- ❋ 2 gallons of gray flat-finish latex paint (see RESOURCES for details)
- ❋ 1 gallon of blue flat-finish latex paint (see RESOURCES for details)
- ❋ Paintbrushes and rollers
- ❋ Gloves
- ❋ Newspaper
- ❋ Pencil
- ❋ Masking tape

1 Lay out your newspaper, open a window for ventilation, and find somewhere else to sleep for the night.

2 Paint all the walls gray.

3 When the paint is thoroughly dry, create a freehand design on the wall with pencil, and go over these lines with masking tape. Be careful getting on and off your chair. It's best for one person to do the top while someone else does the bottom.

4 Once you have finished the design, paint over the tape with a small roller of gray paint until the tape disappears. When that is dry, paint the entire room with the blue paint.

5 Wait at least two hours and then peel off the tape—you've got your cool design.

Other Cool Stuff

We picked up a small gray rug from a carpet store to warm up the floor. It's nice to step on something soft when you get up in the morning.

We made a comforter cover out of two different-color full-size sheets—an easy, cheap way to change the look of the room. Just sew them together inside out like a huge pillowcase, leaving the top open to slip in your old comforter. You can add ribbon ties, too; see page 83 for details.

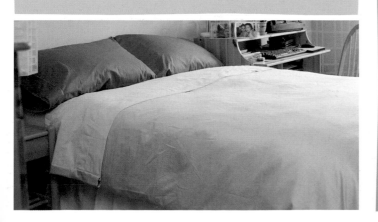

Resources for this Room

❋ ❋ ❋ ❋ ❋ ❋ ❋ ❋

PAINT: Benjamin Moore Pool Party 2059-50 flat-finish latex and Silver Half Dollar 2121-40 flat-finish latex. Krylon spray paint in dark blue, $3 per can.

COOKIE SHEETS: Get the cheap ones; these came from the housewares department at Wal-Mart, $2 each.

SHEETS (for comforter cover): These cost $9 at Kmart.

CD JEWEL CASES: The old reliable 99-cent store has these, about $1 for 5.

PICTURE FRAME: Check out flea markets and thrift shops, or pick up a cheap one at a 99-cent store.

FISH TANKS: These were $8 each at Petland Discount. Check out thrift shops and garage sales for really cheap fish tanks. Clean them out well.

LIGHT CORD: Ours came from Ikea, $7. You can pick one up at any hardware store or lighting supply store.

Chapter Fourteen

Emily's French Flea Market

It was a happy coincidence that we chose a French theme for this chic room. Emily has visited Paris twice, enjoying the museums and the food. She also studies French in school, so we used her French textbook for the phrases on the wall. Emily loves the room and hasn't changed a thing in it. "I spend more time in here now, and it's easy to study," she told us. Her favorite details are the picture frames, in which she can display her postcard collection. Emily's favorite subject in school is architectural drawing, and one day she'd like to study film and photography.

Wall Treatment

Photo Gallery

bonne

Mirror

Paris Lights

Photo Gallery

ooh la la...

Emily had tons of postcards from all over so we decided to make one wall look like the Louvre.

What You'll Need:

* 16 black metal picture frames
* 4 1-yard-long pieces of black ribbon
* 16 pictures or postcards
* Glue gun
* Hammer and nails

1 Secure your pictures or postcards inside the frames.

2 Hot glue four frames to each length of black ribbon. We tied a bow at the top of the ribbon and tacked it to the wall with a small nail.

Table

What You'll Need:

* 1 table
* 1 oval tray
* Spray paint (we used black— see RESOURCES for details)
* Newspaper
* Face mask

1 Make sure your table is clean and dry.

2 Lay down your newspaper, put on your face mask, and spray paint the base of the table black. (Be sure to work in a well-ventilated area, shake the can each time you spray, and keep the can 8 inches from the table's surface.)

3 Paint or decorate the oval tray, if desired. When the paint is thoroughly dry, place it over the table top.

Mirror

What You'll Need:

* 1 mirror
* Pink fabric ribbons and roses
* Black spray paint (see RESOURCES for details)
* Newspaper
* Face mask
* Glue gun

1 Tape a piece of newspaper over the center of your mirror to protect it from the paint. Lay down the rest of your newspaper, put on your face mask, and spray paint the frame black. (Work in a well-ventilated area, shake the can each time you spray, and keep the can 8 inches from the frame's surface.)

2 When the paint is thoroughly dry, glue on some ribbons and roses, and remove the newspaper from the mirror.

Cardboard Bulletin Board

What You'll Need:

* 2 18" x 24" pieces of cardboard
* 1 yard of black-and-white polka dot fabric
* Ribbon
* Masking tape
* Thumbtacks

This is the easiest! Tape the two pieces of cardboard together. Stretch the fabric over the cardboard and tape it to the back. Attach the ribbon with thumbtacks.

Paris Lights

What You'll Need:

* 1 small lamp
* ½ yard of black-and-white polka dot fabric
* Pink fringe, ribbon, roses, lace
* Spray paint (we used hot pink— see RESOURCES for details)
* Newspaper
* Face mask
* Glue gun
* Pencil
* Scissors

1 Remove the lampshade from your lamp. Make sure the lamp is clean and dry. Lay down your newspaper, put on your face mask, and spray paint it hot pink. (Work in a well-ventilated area, shake the can each time you spray, and keep the can 8 inches from the lamp's surface.)

2 Roll the fabric around the lampshade, and trace the pattern. Cut out the pattern, leaving a little extra to tuck under and inside the lampshade. Hot glue the fabric over the existing shade.

3 Glue fringe, ribbon, lace, and roses to the lamp wherever your fancy takes you. *Voilà!*

Candle Holders

What You'll Need:

* Tea pot and/or sugar bowl
* Rice
* Candles
* Spray paint (we used black—see RESOURCES for details)
* Newspaper
* Face mask

1 Remove any stickers from the tea pot and sugar bowl, and make sure they're dry. If you have trouble getting the stickers off, try soaking the pots in warm, soapy water for ½ hour and then scrubbing them off.

2 Lay down your newspaper, put on your face mask, and spray paint the pot and bowl. (Be sure to work in a well-ventilated area, shake the can each time you spray, and keep the can 8 inches from the bowl or pot.) Let dry.

3 Fill the new candle holders with rice and add candles.

NOTE: Never leave a burning candle unattended or within reach of flammable objects like curtains.

Wall Treatment

What You'll Need:

❈ 1 gallon of white flat-finish latex paint (see RESOURCES for details)

❈ 2 gallons of pink flat-finish latex paint (see RESOURCES for details)

❈ 1 quart of black semi-gloss latex paint (see RESOURCES for details)

❈ Paintbrushes, including one small paintbrush for detail work, and rollers

❈ Gloves

❈ Newspaper

❈ Measuring tape

❈ Masking tape

❈ Pencil

1 Lay down your newspaper, open a window, and find somewhere else to sleep for the night.

2 Paint the top half of the walls white.

3 When the paint is dry, tape a horizontal line 50 inches from the floor all the way around the room. Paint all of the area below this line with the pink paint.

4 When the paint is dry, tape off vertical stripes about every 20 inches around the upper white parts of two walls. Paint every other stripe pink; you want to end up with alternating pink and white stripes. Let dry.

5 Put on your gloves and use the black paint to make some decorative squiggles and French phrases around the room (if you don't have a French text-book around, check out the Foreign Phrases section in the back of *Webster's 10th Dictionary* for a nice selection of French words and phrases). Unless you're a skilled painter, it's best to use an erasable pencil to write the words first and then paint over them. We also painted a cat and the Eiffel Tower. Try whatever feels très Français to you!

Other Cool Stuff

To make the comforter prettier, we sewed several light pink ribbon bows in various places. We did the same to the corners of the bench cushion and bed pillows.

We made easy curtains using black-and-white polka dot polyester chiffon. Just follow the directions we gave on page 16.

Resources for this Room

✳ ✳ ✳ ✳ ✳ ✳ ✳ ✳

PAINT: Benjamin Moore Pretty Pink 2077-50 flat-finish latex and Simply White 2143-70 flat-finish latex. For the words and cat we used Benjamin Moore Jet Black 2120-10 in semi-gloss latex. Krylon spray paint in black and hot pink, $3 per can.

RUG: We picked up this small pink rug to match the wall at Target for about $15.

FABRIC FOR CURTAINS: This inexpensive chiffon was only $3 per yard.

TABLE: In New York City everyone puts their unwanted furniture out on the street, so it's an ongoing free flea market. That's where we found this old table base. It had a glass top at one time. Look in thrift shops, flea markets, or in the attic.

FRINGE, RIBBON, LACE, and ROSES: Craft stores will have tons of this stuff for cheap. Don't be afraid to use a lot of it.

CANDLE HOLDERS: These are made from 99-cent store tea pots and sugar bowls.

PICTURE FRAME: These great black metal frames come from Burnes of Boston.

WIRE BENCH and LAMP: We found the bench at a flea market for $5. The lamp came from the Salvation Army, $5. To avoid the possibility of fire, make sure any old lamp you purchase is in good working order.

Chapter Fifteen

Alaia's Royal Treatment

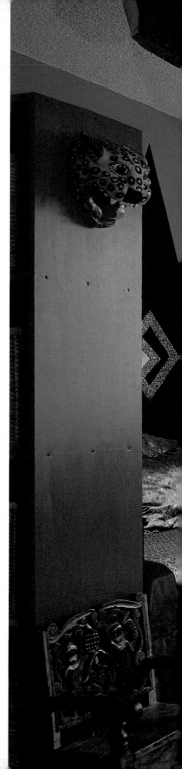

What Alaia most wanted was space separate from her brothers, with whom she shares a big room, so we created an area entirely for her. Alaia says having the new space arranged to her liking helps her tolerate the boys; she couldn't live without music and books in her room, along with her favorite stuffed animals. Alaia enjoys the room's regal feel: "I love anything weird and exotic, and I love foreign things." She also loves having small tables to display her treasures. Alaia likes classical music and rock, especially music by the singer Shakira. Her hobbies include bike riding, karate, and swimming.

Ceiling Drape

Glitter Mirror

Wall Treatment

Lampstorpioco

Glitter Picture Frames

Princess Pillowcase

Princess Pillowcase

What You'll Need:

* 1 standard pillowcase (to use as a pattern)
* 1 standard pillow
* 1 yard of fabric (we used Chinese brocade)
* 1½ yards of ribbon
* Needle and thread

1 Measure the pillowcase to create a pattern. Cut the fabric according to your pattern and sew the pieces together inside-out, leaving one of the short ends open for inserting the pillow.

2 Sew ribbons to each side of the opening so you can tie the case together after inserting your pillow. Use material in different patterns or colors to create interest.

Glitter Mirror

What You'll Need:

* 1 8" x 8" mirror tile
* Spray paint (we used gold—see RESOURCES for details)
* Clear-drying glue (like Elmer's)
* X-acto knife
* Tape
* Shoe-box lid
* Newspaper
* Face mask

1 Tape a square piece of newspaper in the center of the mirror, leaving a two inch border on the edges. Lay down the rest of your newspaper, put on your face mask, and spray paint the edges of the mirror frame gold. (Work in a well-ventilated room. Be sure to shake the can well each time you spray, and keep the can about 8 inches from the surface you're spraying.)

2 When the paint is thoroughly dry, smear the clear-drying glue around the edges, place the mirror in your shoe-box lid, and sprinkle tons of glitter on it.

3 When the mirror is dry, carefully go around the outer edge of the tape with the X-acto knife so the tape doesn't remove the paint and glitter that might be sticking to it. Then remove the tape.

4 Mount the glitter mirror in the center of the diamond wall treatment (see page 126).

glitter picture frame

What You'll Need:

❋ **2 pieces of cardboard (we made ours 5" x 6"—the size will depend on what you want to frame)**

❋ **Glitter**

❋ **Tape**

❋ **Shoe-box lid**

❋ **Clear-drying glue (like Elmer's)**

❋ **Paintbrush (optional)**

❋ **Newspaper**

❋ **Rubber bands**

❋ **X-acto knife**

1 Using an X-acto knife (be careful—these things are SHARP!), cut 2 pieces of cardboard the same exact size. Cut a square in the middle of one of the pieces of cardboard; it should be a bit smaller than the picture you want to frame.

2 Lay down your newspaper. Cover one side of the piece of cardboard with the hole in it with a clear-drying glue. You can spread it on with a paintbrush to make it even or just use your fingers.

3 Put this piece of cardboard in the lid of a shoe box (trust us—you want to avoid making a mess with this stuff), and sprinkle tons of glitter over it. When it's thoroughly dry, tape your picture to the back of the glittery frame and attach the other piece of cardboard to the back by stretching rubber bands around each side.

Ceiling Drape

What You'll Need:

* 10 yards each of red and purple fabric
* Ladder
* Staple gun or small screws and hooks
* Sewing machine or needle and thread (optional)

We used a lot of fabric for this project, but you can get great, cheap fabric for as little as a dollar a yard.

1 Sew the two pieces of fabric together, or, if you don't want to do all the sewing, just leave them as separate pieces. You get more volume and it's easier!

2 Get up on a ladder and staple the fabric to the ceiling (ask your parents first!). Drape the fabric so it flows the way you like. You can also attach the fabric using small screws and hooks, or a curtain rod.

Lampsterpiece

What You'll Need:

* 1 lamp
* Plastic jewels
* Spray paint (we used purple— see RESOURCES for details)
* Newspaper
* Glue gun or other strong glue (like Magic Tac)
* Face mask
* Scissors

1 Remove the lampshade from the lamp. Lay out your newspaper, put on your face mask, and spray paint the base. (Work in a well-ventilated area, remember to shake the can each time you spray, and keep the can about 8 inches from the surface you're spraying.)

2 When the lamp is thoroughly dry, glue on lots of plastic jewels.

3 Using hot glue, re-cover the shade using any leftover bits of fabrics from the room. We used a different fabric on every side of our shade.

4 Cover all the rough edges with trim. You can really go crazy on these lamps—the more stuff, the better.

Wall Treatment

What You'll Need:

❋ 1 gallon of flat-finish latex dark purple paint (see RESOURCES for details)

❋ 2 gallons of flat-finish latex light purple paint (see RESOURCES for details)

❋ Paintbrushes and rollers

❋ Gloves

❋ Newspaper

❋ Measuring tape or long string with weight

❋ Pencil

❋ Masking tape

Purple is the traditional color for royalty.

1 Lay down your newspaper, open a window, and find somewhere else to sleep for the night.

2 Paint the entire room with the light purple paint. Let dry.

3 Decide where you want to put your diamonds. At each place, draw a straight line from the ceiling to the floor. You can use measuring tape or a string and a weight—just tape the string to the ceiling and let it hang to the floor.

4 Lightly mark the line with an erasable lead pencil and then mark the middle of the line. (For example, our ceiling was 8 feet high, so we marked the center at 4 feet.) From this center point, measure out 16 inches to the right and left and 16 inches above and below. Connect these points to form a diamond.

5 Tape around the diamond and paint it in with the dark purple paint. Let dry completely and remove the paint.

Other Cool Stuff

We stapled some extra purple fabric above the window.

We used a great big red bathroom rug as a cool tapestry on the bed, and put lots of comfortable, homemade pillows on the floor so Alaia's friends could feel like royalty, too!

Resources for this Room

❊ ❊ ❊ ❊ ❊ ❊ ❊ ❊ ❊

PAINT: We used Benjamin Moore 2071-50 Light Purple flat–finish latex and 2071-30 Mystical Grape flat–finish latex. Krylon spray paint in gold and purple, about $3 each.

FABRIC: We opted for an inexpensive fabric for the Ceiling Drape, about $2 a yard. The fabric for the pillowcases cost about $4.

RUG (on bed): From Urban Outfitters, $30.

LAMP: We picked up a curvy old lamp at a garage sale for $6. To avoid the possibility of fire, make sure any used lamp is in good working order.

TRIM: Any craft store will have this, and look in the crafts department of Kmart or Target.

MIRROR: An 8" x 8" mirror tile costs about $3 at any hardware store.

Buyer's Guide

✳ ✳ ✳ ✳ ✳ ✳ ✳ ✳

✳ **BED BATH & BEYOND:** A great resource for comforters, pillows, frames, and more. Go to bedbathandbeyond.com.

✳ **BENJAMIN MOORE:** This is the best paint you can buy, and don't you deserve the best? You can even get special mixes if there's a color you'd like to match. Check out their website to see the cool colors that they offer: www.benjaminmoore.com or call 1-888-236-6667 (7 a.m. to 7 p.m. EST).

✳ **BIG LOTS:** This is a remainder 99-cent-style store where you never know what you'll find. Cheap and fun! Go to www.cnstore.com to find a location near you.

✳ **BURNES OF BOSTON:** They make beautiful, long-lasting frames and photo albums in many styles that look great and don't cost that much: www.burnesofboston.com.

✳ **THE CONTAINER STORE:** Need something to put your stuff in? This is the best source for plastic boxes and other put-in-ables to keep your things in line. Go to thecontainerstore.com.

✳ **HOME DEPOT:** They've got just about every kind of hardware item under the sun in one place, so you don't have to schlep around town to find what you need. They even offer home decorating classes. Check out their website: www.homedepot.com

✳ **IKEA:** You can't walk out of this cool store without buying something at a great price that you'll want to paint or decorate yourself. Go to www.ikea-usa.com for more information and a store near you.

✳ **KMART:** Go to www.bluelight.com to see what's on sale at Kmart, a great resource for inexpensive home décor.

✳ **KRYLON:** This is great spray paint. It's easy to use, always dries to a beautiful finish, and is available in a huge range of colors. They have a great website that teaches you how to use spray paint the right way, and there are also a lot of project ideas you might want to try: www.krylon.com.

✳ **LINENS 'N THINGS:** A great resource for cheap sheets and pillowcases that you can also turn into curtains. Go to www.LNT.com

✳ **MICHAEL'S ARTS AND CRAFTS:** A good source for your decorating needs. Click on the Creative Connection to learn about art and how to do some cool projects: www.michaels.com.

✳ **ORIENTAL TRADING COMPANY:** A great, really inexpensive place to get plastic knick-knacks, fans, toys, feather boas, holiday stuff, and more, more, more. Call for a catalog: 1-800-228-2269, or check them out online: www.orientaltrading.com.

✳ **PEARL RIVER:** Check out this New York City Chinese department store's website for cool Asian items like paper lanterns and grass mats: www.pearlriver.com.

✳ **PETLAND DISCOUNT:** This is a regional discount pet supply store; if you live in the greater New York area, it's a great place to pick up fish tanks, not to mention treats for your pet: www.petlanddiscounts.com

✳ **PIER 1:** A great place to get moderately priced furniture, great glassware, and knick-knacks galore. Their website shows you what's new and where to find a store near you: www.pier1.com. Check out their Clearance Store section online.

✳ **THE SALVATION ARMY AND GOODWILL:** Pick up your Yellow Pages, look up Thrift Shops and Clothing—Bought and Sold, write down the phone numbers and addresses, call to confirm what their hours are and what they stock, borrow a car, and get to it, girls! For limited budgets, these stores cannot be beat. Since you're redoing and restoring, a few nicks and scratches won't matter a bit. Just be sure that whatever you buy has working parts and that the quality is at least good (if not very good or excellent). You don't want to commit to hours of painting and adorning only to discover you've got a lamp that's going to fizzle out, or a mirror/table/bench/picture frame that's going to fall apart after a few days. Buyer beware!

✳ **SWIFFER:** We love this new cleaning device that pulls the dust and dirt off decorative touches in your room without hurting the object. Go to www.swiffer.com to learn all about it.

✳ **TARGET:** One of the coolest stores around. Go to www.target.com, and click on their Sale And Clearance section to see what's cheap.

✳ **TREASURE ISLAND:** A great New York-area craft store that's not just for holiday decorating. If you've never been to one of these stores, you don't know what you're missing. They offer craft classes, too. Check out their website for more: www.treasureislandstores.com.

✳ **URBAN OUTFITTERS:** Go to www.urbanoutfitters.com, and click on the Apartment section for cool pillows, comforters, drapes, and other housewares. You can also find a store near you.

✳ **WAL-MART:** A great store to pick up basics that you can rework to turn your room around. Check out their website: www.walmart.com.